# Children and Screen Media in Changing Arab Contexts

Tarik Sabry · Nisrine Mansour

# Children and Screen Media in Changing Arab Contexts

## An Ethnographic Perspective

Tarik Sabry
Department of Media and
Communications
University of Westminster
London, UK

Nisrine Mansour
Communication and Media Research
Institute
University of Westminster
London, UK

ISBN 978-3-030-04320-9     ISBN 978-3-030-04321-6   (eBook)
https://doi.org/10.1007/978-3-030-04321-6

Library of Congress Control Number: 2018967279

Cover illustration: © Melisa Hasan

This Palgrave Pivot imprint is published by the registered company Springer Nature Switzerland AG
The registered company address is: Gewerbestrasse 11, 6330 Cham, Switzerland

*"Don't forget about us when you go back to London!"*
*A 12-year-old Syrian refugee, addressing the ethnographers*
*after the last ethnographic visit in Beirut.*

*This book is dedicated to him.*

# Acknowledgements

Ethnography is an intimately affective and entangled business. In this book, the children were our real teachers: They taught us how to do ethnography intimately—they taught us to listen, observe—they taught us how to un-theorise in order to theorise anew. They taught us phenomenology. We are deeply indebted to all the children and the parents who took part in this ethnographic project. In order to preserve their privacy, all accounts were anonymised, and pseudonyms were used throughout the volume. We thank the Arts and Humanities Research Council (AHRC) for funding our three-year project. Without their grant, this endeavour would not have seen the light of day. We also thank the University of Westminster's Communication and Media Research Institute, the American University of Beirut, the University of Mohammed V (Rabat) for their great support. A special thanks goes to Fauzia Ahmad, Feryal Awan, Christian Fuchs, Naomi Sakr and Jeanette Steemers. We are also indebted to the following organisations for their help with recruiting respondents for the project: Amel, Basma w Zaytouna, Bourj Hammoud Beit El Nour, Al Nour Mosque in Ladbroke Grove, and the Lebanese Maronite Church in Swiss Cottage, London. We are deeply indebted to our informants, Fatima Tazout in Casablanca and Mariam Balhas in Beirut.

# CONTENTS

# LIST OF FIGURES

CHAPTER 1

# Introduction: Arab Children and the Media—Epistemological Topographies of a Nascent Field

**Abstract** The introduction to this volume details the rationale, theoretical, and methodological approaches, and problematics of conducting research on and with children in Arab contexts and the diaspora. The introduction positions Arab child populations within the emerging field of Arab media and cultural studies and in relation to—and critique of—the broader Western-based field of children and media studies. It questions the muddied historical trajectory through which each of the categories of 'Arab', 'child', and 'audiences' is constructed and consolidated in Western and non-Western epistemologies. This critique is set against the major socio-political and cultural changes that are tearing down the foundations of Arab nationalist narratives. It is also set against today's politico-mediascapes that followed the 1990s' technological boom induced by Arab states' liberalisation policies, and which turned Arab populations at home and in exile into the most mediatised populations on the globe. Today's deeper (digital) media penetration has provoked profound and visceral changes to child audiences turned users, in terms of the rapid changes in the array of available screen technology, their varying access to it, and their viewing habits and preferences.

Excerpts of this chapter were published in Mansour, N. (2018). Unmaking the Arab/Muslim Child: Lived Experiences of Media Use in Two Migratory Settings. *Middle East Journal for Culture and Communication, 11*(1), 91–110. Used with permission from Brill Publishers.

The chapter makes the case for articulating new ontological, epistemo-logical, and methodological parameters that allow to clarify what we mean by, and how we engage with, childhoods, Arabness, and related media technologies.

**Keywords** Arab children · Critical theory · Phenomenology · Screen media · Ethnography

## Arab Child Populations in Context(s)

In the summer of 2014, we held a creative workshop with 9- to 12-year-old children in Casablanca with the purpose to understand children's everyday use of screen media. Focusing on world news, researchers and participants engaged in the following discussion:

> *Nisrine*: do you watch the news?
> *Boy 1*: I don't like watching the news, it is all about war and poor children being killed. What is happening to the children in Gaza is horrible.
> *Girl 1*: It makes me very sad, you see blood everywhere, children's remains are scattered across the streets.
> *Nisrine*: So, who is fighting in Gaza?
> *Boy 2*: It is the rebels against the regime.
> (Creative Workshop 4, Casablanca, July 2014)

These recollections threw serious questions as to how we approach researching 'Arab' children and media use in today's devastatingly charged, hyper-mediated, and trans-temporal contexts. It compelled us to wonder, how a child born and bred in Morocco, the farthest corner of the shifting pan-Arab geo-political map, relates to, and understands, the bloodiness of the Israeli–Palestinian conflict. At the time of the field-work, the 2014 Israeli offensive on Gaza confirmed that the conflict remains at the heart of the Arab nationalist cause amid the overlapping layers of more recent conflicts ripping the region.

To give an idea of this overlapping layering, the encounter with the children came at midpoint of our ethnographic inquiry into Arab children's media use, which rolled over three summers between 2013 and 2015 in three contextually disparate sites of London, Casablanca, and Beirut. These three summers of fieldwork were punctuated by the withering euphoria of the Arab revolts and unprecedented escalation of violence in Syria, Yemen, Iraq, and Libya (2013), a major offensive by Israel over Gaza (2014), serial car bombings in Lebanon (2014), and the ravaging effect of the Syrian conflict on its populations, leading to the mass and often deadly exodus of refugees on the shores of Europe (2015). As these seismic events are wrapping the Arab region, their impact on children's experiences and views of the world tend to be over-looked as Sonia Livingstone (2002: 25) pointed in the *Young People New Media Project*:

> Rather than see children as the object of media effects, they are instead seen as actors in the household and community, co-constructors of the meanings and practices of their everyday lives. Indeed, if we forget to see young people as actors as well as acted upon, if we fail to listen to partic-ipants' voices as they speak for themselves...we miss understanding their experience of the media, tending to succumb to our often-nostalgic per-spective on childhood and so missing the new skills and opportunities that these media may open for them.

There is no doubt that the Arab region is going through major socio-po-litical and cultural changes that are tearing down the foundations of nationalist narratives that made up the post-colonial raison d'être of Arab nationalism. These violent changes are remodelling national, religious, and cultural identities. Palestine used to be the beacon of a regional Arab national identity embraced by succeeding generations across the Arab region as they grew up under nationalist regimes that championed the Palestinian cause as the heart of their often autocratic raison d'être. In the early phase of the dispossession of Palestinians, tensions between and within Arab nations were pushed under the carpet of a unified front in the fight against the forceful establishment of Israel in 1948. Following several defeats and victories, Arab states gradually broke and warmed up to Israel with peace accords struck in Egypt (1979), Morocco (1994), and Jordan (1994), and trade relations established in Gulf countries.[1] These peace accords brought overarching state narratives of non-interven-tionism, crushing overt political engagement, and any official narratives of solidarity of their populations with the Palestinian cause. More recent conflicts and destabilisation by regional and international players, such as the US, Europe, Russia, Turkey, Iran, and Gulf countries, resulted in the rise of Islamist military ideologies  that fragmented narratives of Muslim unity for Palestine—the other prime marker of Arab nationalism. The recent Arab revolts and the toppling (or near toppling) of long-standing dictators also uncovered an enduring malaise about decades of oppression and grievances that older and younger generations have endured for periods as long as 42 years in some cases, as in the example of Ghaddafi's Libya, or the long-established (near) absolutist governance models of Gulf countries. The ravaging instability following from them added layers of complexity and incoherence to an already charged and fractured Arab identity.

In parallel to political hegemony, Arab regimes have actively and systematically imposed neo-liberal frameworks of economic governance, with deep effects on populations. In the decade preceding the recent Arab revolts, several regimes gradually dropped their socialist/statist approaches that provide public services and subsidies. As early as the 1990s, Mobarak's Egypt led the way in liberalising markets. Assad's Syria and Ghaddafi's Libya followed suit in the 2000s, joining other countries with historically liberal economic frameworks, such as Morocco, Lebanon, and Jordan. Policies included deregulation and privatisation of public institutions and services including education, health, and transport, as well as public spaces such as commercial districts and coastlines. The privatisation of public life has widened the gap between the rich and the poor.

## Socio-Political Contexts Meet Technological Advances

Within these seismic geo-political changes, Arab children today are greatly under scrutiny. They are feared both as potential victims and as fuel for armed conflicts and violent ideologies. They are a swelling and vocal demographic that is stirring local and international governance and mediatic unease. Those living in the Arab region are posing a threat to the imposing regimes. Those in the diaspora are forming a critical political mass that is confronting the hypocrisy of exclusionary and racist Western values. Those fleeing conflicts in exodus (mainly to Europe) are stripped of their internationally recognised humanitarian protection rights and considered instead as walking bomb threats. However, the limitations of these macro-political analyses cannot be missed. They beg the question as to the validity and usefulness of blanketing some 135 Million children (World Bank 2017) (excluding the diaspora) living in 22 Arab countries with disparate histories, socio-political conditions, and cultural practices under the monolithic category of 'Arab' identity that has been imposed by Western and Arab epistemologies. This questioning is particularly timely since the recent changes have induced a jagged sedimentation of mediated narratives of Arab existence in a hyper-globalised and trans-temporal world.

This scrutiny has also at its heart the ways in which Arab populations, including children, are engaging with the significant changes pertaining to media technology globally and regionally. Today's children are growing up in what could be dubbed as the post-satellite boom era that swept the region in the 1990s and which was aptly exemplified in the 'Al Jazeera Phenomenon' (Mansour 2018). The 1990s technological boom marking Arab screen media was a game changer in terms of production and content, as well as access to and use of screen media. Several Arab regimes gave way to globalisation by gradually—if reluctantly—liberalising their broadcasting policies (Sakr 2002). Arab mediascapes saw a fundamental transformation from state monopoly of highly regulated (read censored) national outlets towards a flourish in popularisation, privatisation, and regionalisation (Sakr 2007).

In addition to breaking the monopoly of state media narratives over populations, this media boom had one particular—if overlooked—characteristic. It turned Arab populations at home and in exile into the most mediatised populations on the globe. Unlike other corners of the globe, the digital boom resulted in the deepest inter-penetration of satellite broadcasting. Arabic-language broadcasts ranked 6th most used language on satellite TV globally with 73% of them available as free to air (Amezaga Albizu 2007). They also had an expansionist outlook, with 30% aimed outside Arab countries. Europe was their main target with the highest share of 120 broadcasts, positioning Arabic-speaking broadcasts as the largest non-European language captured in Europe (Amezaga Albizu 2007). In reverse penetration, the Arab region disproportionately received the highest numbers of English-speaking broadcasts than any other region globally. It received 318 US-based channels directed to the Mediterranean and West Asia, preceding their European reach of 305 broadcasts (Amezaga Albizu 2007).[2] While two-thirds of these broadcasts were encrypted, loose regulation on private providers in Arab countries resulted in large scale encryption piracy of these channels, making them widely accessible at no extra cost (Mansour 2018).

Thirty years on, the primacy of satellite broadcasters remains the main analytical lens in studying Arab children and media use despite the significant advances in screen—and particularly—digital/online media. Of course, notable exceptions relate to Arab youth's use of digital media in the Arab uprisings, although they remain within a narrow and heavy focus on practices and narratives of politicisation and radicalisation. This focus misses out on the more profound and visceral changes pertaining to audiences turned users, in terms of the rapid changes in the array of available screen technology, children's varying access to it, and their viewing habits and preferences. Most importantly, the affective formations of childhood through media use as well as the everyday processes of subjectification within and beyond politicisation amid these charged contexts are yet to be explored.

In order to analyse the ontological, epistemological, and methodological parameters governing the field of Arab children and media use, it is useful to trace the genealogies of the field of media studies that established the dominant narratives on what we mean by, and how we engage with, childhoods, Arabness, and related media technologies.

## Locating Arab Children Within/Out the Field of Media Studies

Tracing back the historical birth of Western screen media indicates how the field of media studies preoccupied itself with its own context—without naming it as one—before spreading to the rest of the world. In other words, it started as an exercise in understanding the consolidation of Western societies and systems as they were evolving through, and struggling with, industrialisation and modernity. At the time, as most of the rest of the world (to borrow from Partha Chaterjee 2003) was still colonised, it was largely discounted from inquiry. Instead, early Western scholarly attention focused inwards, towards Western societies connected through the communication technologies of the time, the phone, radio, and TV (and later on to online screens), which propelled their societies into the era of late modernity. It was the first step into the era of virtual communication and it threw important questions as to its seductive and pervasive power at the levels of the individual and collective imaginative, aesthetic, material, and dogmatic control.[3] As Western societies grappled with the new beast that emerged from the industrial revolution, one central question preoccupied early scholarship: How to understand, optimise, and protect technicalised societies—individuals and groups—as they engaged with the popularisation of media and communication.

Systems of Western governance were driven by the goal of economic standardisation of individuals and groups. This produced a chain reaction of scholarly fields that were meant to study and promote this goal. As the foundations of the fields of sociology, psychology, linguistics, and economics were set, their combination gave birth to communication studies, which in turn branched into the fields of media studies and cultural studies. Growing from a mosaic of disciplines, media studies is a relatively nascent field compared to other social sciences and humanities disciplines and still struggles to impose its authority as a distinct field of study (Buckingham 2008). It is a field that evolved from various sociological and psychological traditions such as positivism, Marxism, symbolic interactionism, and cultural studies.

The birth of communication as an industry coincided with the historical moment of the interbellum period between the First and Second World Wars. The central role that media and communication played in the rise of capitalist advertising in the US, nationalist propaganda in Nazi Germany, and Soviet Russia was undeniable. American functionalist theorists flagged the threat of socialist and nationalist propaganda that numbs people in the same way as a hypodermic needle would. Marxist and critical theorists denounced them as capitalist structures intended to tame the masses and lure them into the false promise of unattainable, standardised, material happiness. These two antithetical theories had one commonality. They both exposed the power of the media in/as propaganda, or the ability to influence populations through mediated ideas. Functionalists considered that the media, if uncontrolled, could fuel the populations' thirst to social ills such as prostitution, drugs, and fragmentation of social values resulting from modernity.

In short, while modernity was inevitable and desirable for a prosperous society, populations—turned into audiences—were not to be trusted with reaping its benefits. Audiences were considered rather irrational by nature and, if left to their own devices, would constitute a threat to social cohesion in democratic Western regimes. This logic claimed that, since democratic Western regimes unquestionably valued freedoms and liberties, society's ills meant that populations' behaviours were at fault. Conversely, critical theorists placed the blame on the capitalist structures underpinning the media industry that tie populations into false consciousness through media uses. Populations were gullible and in need for control. Despite the philosophical departures of these two antithetical theories, they both focused on human behaviour in analysing the media. For functionalists, the problematic relationship between the media and the masses did not stem from the sender of the message, since they perceived their system of political and economic governance, embodied in the US and British systems, as epitomising freedom and democracy. The problem lay in the behaviour of the masses, who were deemed irrational and driven to deviance. So, for them, the discipline was to focus on how to monitor audiences' behaviour and optimise the effect of the self-proclaimed democratic state and free economic forces. For critical theorists, the problem lay in the capitalist system of the media, which reduces people's reactions to chasing chimeric notions of consumerist happiness.

Both theories were concerned with the dangerous blanket effect of the media on populations. They both similarly conceptualised audiences as 'masses'. Functionalists resorted to understanding how audiences are affected by the media by reducing individual and group dynamics to behaviourism. Marxist/critical theorists sought to critique the rise of 'mass culture', whereby capitalist elite broadcasters and/or dictatorship regimes indoctrinated audiences and lured them into consumerist behaviour (see Adorno and Horkheimer 1972 [1944]; Fuchs 2016, 2017). They also both converged over an underlying positivist approach that analyses audiences' behaviour and everyday cultural practices as passive and subject to the outdated effects model. This attention to human behaviour within the two contrasting bodies of scholarship has its roots in the late enlightenment meta-discourse on modernity that aligned social sciences with natural sciences to construct the formation of the modern subject. From Darwin, we learned that we evolved from animals, drawing on our instincts and reflexes to survive. From Marx, we learned that our material relation with labour and *technicalisation* of exchange value determined the evolution of (Western) society. It was also the time that saw the birth of quantifying our instincts and our labour. It followed from the birth of economics and statistics as ways to count populations. As Foucault (1978) asserts, economy started not as a discipline to study material/labour relations between people, but as a tool to count populations and quantify them by household, resources, and activities.

It was a time where statistics were considered a tool to quantify all aspects of populations' existence. That is why the field of economics was earlier named 'political economy', marking the dialectic relationship between materiality and governance. As populations became quantifiable through statistics, psychology and politics were elevated to the realm of the sciences at the start of the twentieth century. The analysis of the self gradually moved away from Freudian introspective, if problematic methods of analysis, towards tracing patterns of quantifiable behaviour, using rational and empirical methods that favoured quantitative and standardised methods similar to the natural sciences. The self was stripped of the 'contextual' and constructed into a 'universalist' behavioural framework of analysis. Populations' behaviour became a central scholarly concern. Behaviourism in psychology and behaviouralism in political science both reduced populations to individualist basic reactive behaviour, even extending to analysing their thoughts and dreams, with the main purpose to predict their voting behaviour. It is important to note here that both schools of thought, the functionalists and Marxist/critical theorists, used the hermeneutics of suspicion as a default position for critiquing modernity and its institutions. Hermeneutics of suspicion has also been extended to engage with notions of everyday life. Totalising accounts of the everyday drew much from French structuralism; to be precise, from Althusser, the 'Pope of structuralist Marxism', where, as we learn from Paddy Scannell, 'lived experience cannot be taken as the ground for anything because it is unconscious in a double sense: it is unreflective … and therefore gives no account for itself. And it is also unconscious in psychoanalytical terms, and therefore cannot account for itself' (Scannell in Sabry 2007: 12). In this volume, we argue that positioning the everyday and lived experience along this line of thought clearly limits what can be said about cultural experience and certainly has serious implications for the ways in which the media and their audiences are interpreted. For us, a more nuanced critique of the everyday has to combine ideological critique with a more culturalist/anthropological positioning. We take our cue from scholars such as Raymond Williams ("culture is ordinary"), who takes lived experience as the ground for a conscious and reflective analysis of culture. In fact, we go further than this in the book by adopting a phenomenological approach as a default position for thinking about Arab children and their media uses. Here, we take our cue from media phenomenologist Paddy Scannell who in *Television and the Meaning of Live* (2014), asserts that phenomenology is as:

[F]irmly committed to a view that thinking begins by looking outwards not inwards. In an originary sense we are moved (are summoned) to thinking by looking at the world, the alpha and Omega of all thought – where thinking begins and ends... This means to attempt to think of things in their terms in the first place: not what *I* might think they are but what, in fact, *they* are. (Scannell 2014: 5)

We are, we need to add, also hugely influenced by what Alasuutari called "the third generation" of reception studies (1999) that built on Stuart Hall's encoding/decoding approach including Morley (1980, 1986), Radway (1984) and Ang (1985). This approach, as we learn from S. Elizabeth Bird (2003: 5), 'acknowledges the very real problems associated with trying to separate text/audience from the culture (and we add the *worldliness*) in which they are embedded'.

## Western Institutions of Authority and Definitions of Child Audiences/Users

Childhood has been mainly conceptualised into two dominant dichotomies of being and becoming that revolve around discourses of fear and hope. In child psychology, the paradigm of hope dates back to the enlightenment and the romantic era and conceptualises children in two different ways. Following Locke, the child is a tabula rasa, or blank slate, which, with proper training and apprenticeship, could develop into blooming adulthood (Awan 2016). A different, more optimistic take was that of Rousseau who considered children not blank slates, but angelic-like pure and innocent beings, who need protection from the tarnishing of adulthood and its corrupting authority (Awan 2016). A third extremist view saw children as volatile pre-social beings, loose cannons in need to be controlled, tamed, and coached into becoming social adults. This view derives from the Christian idea that upholds the natural 'wickedness' of children, and the need for 'correction' to tame them into becoming adults (Gittins 2009: 41–42; Jenks 2009). Perpetuated by the Church, this view justified the birth of compulsory schooling and the rise of the 'cane' as a symbol for discipline in the education system in the eighteenth century (Awan 2016, citing Heywood 2001; Hendrick 1997; Cunningham 1995).

Scholarship on childhood combined these two views and generally understood children as pure—albeit incomplete—beings, giving rise to the hope and fear paradigms. Children's purity established the hope paradigm. With careful guidance and nurturing, children could acquire the foundations of a blossoming and stable adult life. On the other hand, children's incompleteness and unformed beingness also made them impressionable, putting them in need to be guarded from preying adults. Research focused on the process by which children become adults, and the structural and institutional factors affecting this becoming, such as family, class, and closer to our interest, TV, and more recently, the internet.

The fear paradigm is firmly rooted in the effects model, where media are perceived to affect children in particular, with the earliest contributions known as the Payne Fund studies in the 1920s–1930s in the USA. Although the validity and representativeness of these studies were questioned, they strongly shaped public discourse around media and child audiences and formed the seeds for media regulation in the US (Rodman 2004). Central to this fear approach was a moralistic questioning of the changing social dynamics and values induced by modernity, in relation to what was considered then a gullible and impressionable mass population.

It is important to disentangle these contemporary current views and trace their conceptual origins. Several historical studies point that the birth of communication studies, which paved the way to media studies, coincided with the period where children were also reconceptualised through three mechanisms: (1) Standardisation of children's psychology as behaviourism, (2) enlightenment ideas about the natural sciences, and (3) the rise of modern education (Marshall 1989, citing Foucault on formal education).

Hope and fear are intimately related to the enlightenment project which, growing from advances in experimental natural sciences and Darwin's evolution theory, conceptualised human beings as essentially social animals. The birth of communication studies in the US that paved the way to media studies was a time 'children' were also reconceptualised. Standardisation of children's psychology through early experiments, mixed with (1) enlightenment ideas about the natural sciences with (2) the rise of formal education as a way to institutionalise children into future workers (Deacon and Parker 1995).

Two pioneering examples set the basis for scholarly interest in behaviour in both poles of the Western/industrialised world. The first one took place in 1901 in Russia, where Pavlov conducted experiments to study ways of generating classical conditioning in dogs. Pavlov was the first to draw the relationship between biological and mental stimuli. When dogs were presented with food, they biologically drooled. Pavlov introduced the mental stimulus of the bell along with the food. Dogs gradually identified the sound of the bell with appetite, and they drooled even if the food was not there. Pavlov thus discovered one aspect of influence over the animalistic self, that of the promise of desirable outcomes even if they do not materialise. In 1907, in the US, John B. Watson conducted the Kerplunk Experiment studying stimulus and response on rats by placing them in a maze. Watson discovered the embodiment of conditioning, where with enough learning time, rats internalised voluntary motor responses to conditioned response. Watson got further inspired by Pavlov and followed with the infamous "Little Albert Experiment". Watson hypothesised that fear was an innate response within human beings. He went on to experiment with the conditioning of fear within children by triggering fear through loud noises and associating them with innocuous objects like furry objects/puppets. Hence, with this turn into conceptualising Western children and adults as purely biological/behavioural beings, they were epistemologically stripped from their context. The contextual influences were minimised until the development of Marxist theory which conceptualised context purely in the form of socio-economic class differentials, and Max Weber's (2015 [1902]) notion of status. Thus, sociology was the lens for analysis of Western contexts, which perceived it as devoid of 'culture'. Culture was reserved for the study of non-Western subjects, through anthropology (Fabian 1983), which is deeply rooted in colonial systems of governance. Thus, the cultural lens was unwittingly adopted by scholars who wished to overturn the dominant Western social lens for analysis. Scholarly approaches towards white and non-white research child subjects have retained this long-standing bias. Western scholarship primarily analyses Western child audiences from a sociological lens, while it scrutinises non-white children's practices from a cultural lens.

## INTERNATIONALISING AS ARABISING: CHILDHOOD AND MEDIA USE

Scholarship on Arab children and the media is trapped in three types of epistemological and methodological modalities. The dominant one is the victimisation narrative, primarily reflected in the studies on

Palestinian childhood. The other side of the spectrum conceptualises child audiences through the lens of extremism and radicalisation, which was popularised in the counter-terrorism discourse since 9/11. The third modality diverts from an overly political focus. Instead, it engages with the topic from an essentialist anthropological, sociological, and psychological conceptualisations of child development (see Awan 2016). Two main narratives dominate this strand. The first is behavioural approaches to child development that speak of Arab children in totality, extrapolating, for example, from a village in the North of Yemen to epistemological constructions of 'Arab childhood' (Dorsky and Stevenson 1995). The second narrative is a revisionist approach, departing from the Western-influenced frameworks. It conceptualises Arab children within two intersecting analytical lenses, the Islamic legal-institutional lens; and the Arab family traditions and moralistic lens (see Awan 2016). This narrative looks into the rights of the child in Islamic law, and the institutional legal and family settings as Arab countries within an overarching timeless legal and institutional framework of Islamic law in its broadest sense. It is mixed with an 'Arab family' lens that encapsulates the values, norms, and traditions of a 'mono' Arab culture.

Arab-based scholarship picked up on the phenomenon by scrutinising screen media.[4] It was feared as a disruptive force that might corrupt the social fabric and pedagogic moralities used to raise Arab children (Dashty 2010). In particular, Disneyfication was considered a threat to the long-standing moralities of 'Arab traditions' and 'Muslim values' (examples include al-Mesfer, n.d.). These notions were used as overarching categories, with little exploration of the specific processes shaping identity formation. These categories were desirable albeit vague frameworks of childhood modelled after fixed notions of adulthood. Children were indirect objects of study; they featured only as passive recipients of media messages. These accounts followed the early moral panic model found in Western scholarship (see Critcher 2008; Drotner 1999; Messenger Davies 2008).

In Western-driven epistemologies, interest in the role of screen media in Arab children's identity formation rose following the shock of 9/11. As the global 'counterterrorism' discourse gained currency, it allowed for the politicisation of Arab children as victims of or actors in transnational violence. In the Arab region and the diaspora, research used this lens in two contexts: the rise of al-Qa'eda and the escalation of the Israeli–Palestinian conflict.

Research on Palestinian children and the media is a case in point. Palestinian media expressed fear over preserving and fostering children's national identity. In a critical account of this trend, Awan (2016) found that Palestinian children under Israeli occupation were predominantly conceptualised as passive victims threatened with the loss of their national identity. Hence, child-focused screen media productions primarily sought to address this threat. As a result, television content, as well as the pool of research analysing it, was filled with pedagogic messages on 'Palestinianhood' as a driving principle relating to every aspect of children's lives (Awan 2016).

However, Palestinian children were scrutinised following their crucial role in the second intifada (2000–2005) and the ensuing erection of the separation wall around the West Bank by the Israeli government. They became the object of study, not as victims, but rather as potential perpetrators.[5] The inquiry looked inwards, towards Palestinian children (commonly referred to as Arab Israelis) living within Israeli borders. Research focused on comparing Jewish and Arab Israeli children's levels of, and potential for, trauma and violence as a result of their exposure to mediated and non-mediated aspects of the Israeli–Palestinian conflict (Lazovsky 2007; Slone et al. 2011; Lemish and Pick-Alony 2014). Adhering to the media effects approach, this literature sought to inquire into the psyche of Arab Israeli children, only to find few variations between these two groups of children.

In the diaspora, the shock of 9/11 triggered a similar rise in research on Arab child audiences in the same framework of potential victims or perpetrators. The focus was on Arab American children and families in relation to issues of language and social integration, with hints about their religiosity (examples include Saloom 2005; Haboush 2007; al-Salmi and Smith 2015). This body of literature was the first to link Arab diasporic youth with Islamic identity following the discourse of the 'war on terror' and the rise of hybrid Arab and Islamic militant groups. The archetypal profile for this categorisation was al-Qa'eda's leader Osama bin Laden, an Arab (Saudi) national who branded a violent Islamic ideology from a non-Arab (i.e., an Afghani) stronghold.

European scholarship adopted this hybrid categorisation and took it a step further. In the British context, prior to 7/7, there was no systematic research on Muslim child audiences. Following the 7/7 attacks on the London underground in 2005, research started to look into Muslim child audiences. As none of the four alleged attackers was Arab, research turned to assess the 'Muslim threat', rather than inquiring about the contradictions it implied in relation to the British colonial legacy (examples include Meer 2007; Scourfield et al. 2013).[6] Research in other European contexts, such as the Netherlands and France, followed suit (Buijzen et al. 2007; Rinnawi 2012; Leurs 2015). Given that the majority of the migrant populations were North African, the analytical category of 'Arab' disappeared. Research conflated 'Arab' and 'Muslim' identities' and Arab diasporic youth became 'Muslim' by default. Thus, Arab children and young audiences at home and in the diaspora were further compacted into essentialised notions of being and becoming that revolve around the 'potential Islamic terrorist child'. As these analytical categories were conflated, the implications of such teleological epistemologies could not be overlooked. Under this uniform 'Muslim' category, there was no room to account for the vast diversity of childhood experiences. Nor was there any articulation of the role of interconnected ecologies in shaping the processes of meaning-making across variables of nationality, ethnicity, class, upbringing practices, education frameworks, socio-political environments, and connectivity infrastructure.

In examining the genealogy of media studies, child audiences/users, and Arabness, one finds that the contemporary epistemologies are composed of a historical sedimentation of sweeping narratives that assume to speak for—rather than with—the experiences of the populations they intend to study. They favour dominant Western-centric political economy/production approaches that conceptualised non-Western child audiences/users into fixed orientalist constructions of childhoods in isolation of the interdependence between human experiences, everyday life, and media technology.

## THEORETICAL AND METHODOLOGICAL FRAMEWORK FOR AN ALTERNATIVE READING OF ARAB CHILDREN AND MEDIA USE

This book aims to challenge these established epistemological narratives and offers a shift in the way we research and understand Arab children and the media in the twenty first century at several analytical levels. First, there is a need to reverse the top-down approach to child audiences, which favoured political economy and quantitative analyses over qualitative, anthropologically led ones. Some important exceptions are worth noting first, including the work of David Buckingham who stayed faithful to cultural studies' conjunctional method, championing the triangular study of text, production, and children audiences (see Buckingham 2008; Buckingham et al. 1999; Buckingham and Bragg 2004; Buckingham and Sefton-Green 1994; Buckingham 2002). Exceptions aside, these established top-down narratives rely on a double-bind, artificial divide between a media-centric and anthropocentric approaches, as well as the schism in analysing media in terms of the seemingly innocuous 'old' media, and the threat of 'new' media. More often than not, the media-centric approaches ignore the wider and very important socio-cultural and political contexts in which children's media uses take place. Our ethnographic and non-media-centric approach, inspired by both the cultural studies (see Morley 1992; Moores 1993) and phenomenological method (Scannell 2014) has unconcealed for us conjunctional and meaningful connections between children's media uses, *habitus* and *worldliness* we had not foreseen. Our aim has been to develop an ethnographic approach that recognises the evolving nature of media technology and the symbiotic, inherently political, interconnectedness between media and audiences'/users' experiences and perceptions of the world. The reason for this strategy relates to the epistemological turn that we are experiencing within not only the age of globalised yet fractured late modernity but also in understanding the trajectory of human communication. Our times reflect fundamental changes in human communication, with the advent of screen and particularly digital technology. The concern with 'new' media today is mostly due to the profound inter-generational changes in media use, in terms of both economics and politics of technological inventions and spread. However, these changes are not exceptional to this age. Rather, they are akin to the invention of the then new media technological advances such as the telephone or the television, or indeed, the ancient invention of alphabetical script. Thus, it is important to position the inquiry within a historically relevant framework that acknowledges the non-linearity of social trajectories, and approach it in ways that expose the genealogies of the dominant narratives on childhood and media use. This is of particular relevance since childhood is by default a fundamental universal experience of a life course shared by all humans. It thus encapsulates human imagination of pasts and futures, origins, and destinations. The experiences of children in the Arab region need to be articulated within both the meta-intense changes gripping the Arab region, and the broader global interconnections of digitised future generations experiencing glocalised everyday experiences.

To have a comprehensive scope of these experiences, there is a need to reassess how we study the overarching processes of meaning-making that transpire from children's engagement with the media. One level is to inquire about their current engagement with the changing mediascapes. Another level is to locate this engagement within the sedimented layers of media and narratives of nationalism, identity, allegiance, perpetration, victimhood, moralities passed on through the older generations as well as the established regimes of governance they live in. These narratives have been mainly championed by adults, based on their own fears and hopes towards imagined futures that are driven by the incoherent demands of late modernity, colonialism, and capitalism.

Most importantly, we think it imperative to drive the inquiry towards narratives that are most important to children—those of growing up, childhood, existence, beliefs, practices, authority, learning, aspirations, futures, and *worldliness*. One fundamental concern relates to the momentous changes pertaining to children's mediated assemblages of what we can call 'toolboxes of existence' or media as *equipment* (see Chapter 5). These mediated assemblages are equipping children with new networks that shape their knowledge acquisition, material value formation, engagement with authority, and moralities around belonging and identity. Another crucial concern is to understand the profound changes in the ecologies of mediated sensation, taste, and connectedness with their physical, social, cultural, and political environment.

The core of the proposed inquiry is about reconciling anthropological, phenomenological, and media-centred approaches both conceptually and methodologically. This is possible by fundamentally reconsidering the established divide between anthropo-centric and media-centric approaches. This divide is based on the narrow definition of the media as an invention of the modernity project since enlightenment. It assumes that humans predated the media which they invented. In fact, media predate modernity. They have always been part of human experience, and they cannot be dissociated from humans' desire and necessity to communicate with their environment and making sense of their existence.

Here, there is a need to attend to some largely overlooked conceptualisations of human communication that restore the indivisibility between humans and their natural and social environments. Humans are able to make sense of the world they live in primarily through their senses. The controversial take of McLuhan (1994 [1964]) in his work on media as extension of the senses offers a useful starting point as the human body is reconceptualised as a sensory receptor of input from the surrounding environment. These sensations are translated in the mind through a process of meaning-making that transcends language and extends the semiotic and affective realms.

The central inquiry in this book is about bridging concepts and methods in understanding this intricate link between humans and the media. It utilises the crossovers between ethnography phenomenology and cultural studies to excavate counter-narratives of Arab childhood and media use, both in terms of lived experiences and mediated narratives and processes of meaning-making and the possibilities that open up as a result. It also reconciles ethnography with media archaeology through the analogy of mediated performativity. This concept offers a point of departure that recognises, and values, the indivisibility of mediation between mind and body. It borrows the anthropo-centric framework of the body/theatre/performativity/spectacle, which is best served by ethnography. It also restores the validity of the framework of media histories/archaeology that is concerned with the pre- and post-cinematic media/imagery/sensations. In this phenomenological approach, the everyday is reconceptualised as mediated theatre where both sensations and imageries of theatre and cinema are sedimenting. It allows to reveal the layers of memory and imagination of existence and futures.

## On Methods and Ethics

The present volume is the fruit of a three-year AHRC-funded project, *Orientations in the Development of Screen Media for Arabic-Speaking Children (Initial Title: Orientations in the Development of Pan-Arab*

*Television for Children).* The project initially set out to investigate changes in the creation, commercialisation, and reception of pan-Arab television for children. Thus, the research was designed to work simultaneously on production, distribution, and reception of Arabic-language programming targeted at 7- to 12-year-old child audiences via satellite. With this focus, it sought to achieve a holistic understanding of trajectories of change in this field. This objective called for overlapping and integrated analyses of: (a) the political economy of production and distribution of children's screen-based media; (b) the purposes of children's screen-based media as negotiated between competing elites; and (c) the cultures of reception among young Arabic-speaking viewers in Arab countries and the UK. This involved a multi-method, three-pronged approach designed to explore institutions, programming, and audiences.

In this sense, the project sought to align the three main epistemological poles of media studies, namely production studies and its heavy focus on political economy, textual analysis focusing on representations, and audience studies with its anthropologically driven approach. In practice, the project team operated within three different epistemological and geographic worlds of cultural and knowledge production reflected in the fieldwork design. The process of creation and distribution of children-focused programmes took place in UAE and Qatar, which constitute the hub for Arabic-speaking child-focused broadcasting, and the UK, which held some of the largest production partnerships with them. The programming strand was reserved to the Palestinian case, to be investigated through doctoral research. The use of media by Arab children was conducted in the UK, Lebanon, and Morocco. The methodological selection of the field countries for the audience research primarily respected the comparative factor between Arabic-speaking respondents in the British diaspora and in-home countries. Another major concern was the relative stability of the selected home country in the midst of the Arab uprisings' precarious security situation during the running of the project (2013–2015).

With the start of the fieldwork in 2013, the three production, content, and reception strands ran their own field research in parallel, exchanging knowledge through periodic steering committee meetings and related symposia organised by the team. The initial methodological approach for the project (as its initial title suggested), centred around Pan-Arab broadcasting due to the dominance of Pan-Arab satellite broadcasting in the region as well as related academic literature.

The production and content analysis strands remained focused on broadcasters (national, regional, and UK-based production partners), pointing to interesting findings about the disconnect content creators and production managers had with the broad child audience population in both the Arab region and the diaspora.

Similarly, as we embarked on the audience research strand, the main focus of this book, we initially adopted a pan-Arab TV-centred approach. However, with the early steps of the field research, we realised that the media practices of Arabic-speaking children both at home and in the diaspora exceeded academic and broadcasters' assumptions and expectations. Child respondents across class, gender, ethnicity, and geographies have fully embraced multi-platform screen media on par with their peers in other Western and non-Western contexts. Another realisation related to the interpenetration of the traumatic effects of the spiralling conflicts as well as sensitivity to the rising climate of Islamophobia across child respondents and their families at home and diaspora. Thus, we endeavoured to account fully for their experiences in the fieldwork and analysis within three sets of ethical parameters.

The first parameter relates to our ethical duty towards the child respondents as minors exposed (directly or mediatically) to conflicts and stereotyping, and who depend on their parents' consent to participate in the research. In order to secure respondents' consent, we approached parents with a clear and detailed pledge to respect children's anonymity and well-being at all stages of the research from fieldwork to publication of the findings. In addition, we sought to secure consent from the children themselves in advance by explaining to them the purpose of the research in a simple yet uncompromising language, clearly giving them the option to opt out at any time. We also pledged to anonymise the names of child respondents and their families and substituted them with pseudonyms throughout data capture, analysis, and publication as is the case with the present volume.

Second, in order to optimise children's well-being and minimise traumatic encounters, we designed fieldwork activities in the least invasive way possible. As such, we moved away from direct questioning and scrutiny of media practices and towards a more socially conscious and playful approach that revolves around their interests and preferences. We also designed research activities not only to make them 'fun' and 'engaging'. Rather, our purpose was to develop innovative methods and tools that foster a child development approach through creative and artistic practices that value children's time and effort.

Third, we streamlined this approach across the three methodological tools adopted in the design, namely creative workshops, viewing diaries, and ethnographic visits which were tailored to each of the three field sites. The creative workshops included collage and drawing activities such as the *tree of life* where participants would identify their roots, qualities, and hopes for the future. In addition, they engaged in a simulation exercise where they acted as the founders of a multi-platform media channel for children and set out to design their own viewing schedule from scratch. The viewing diaries included, in addition to a simple record of their media practices, exploratory themes around their favourite activities, their connections with their loved ones, and their hopes for their future. The ethnographic visits involved largely unstructured social and play time spent with the children and their families. Together we watched shows, played games, listened to music, and exchanged jokes and insights on the idiosyncrasies of everyday 'Arabness' that brought us all together.

These ethnographic encounters between 2013 and 2015 interweaved the playfulness of summer holidays among child respondents, their parents' ongoing pursuit of a decent living among often tight socio-economic realities, and the most intense acceleration of turbulence wrapping the Arab region. The London fieldwork (2013) marked the end of euphoria of the 'Arab Spring' with the military takeover in Egypt, and the escalation of conflict in Syria, Iraq, Libya, and Yemen. The Casablanca fieldwork (2014) took place amid the Israeli offensive on Gaza. The Beirut fieldwork (2015) was carried out at the time of the mass exodus of Syrian refugees to Europe and terror bombings in Beirut. These seismic events reverberated across the three Arab and European contexts with some of the heaviest emotional implications on the respondents, their families, and us—the researchers. In order to protect child respondents and their families from further psychological harm, we decided not to probe them on the subject, and to engage with it only if and when it came up. As a result, discussions of sensitive topics amounted to a fraction of the wealth of data generated in the process.

It is an understatement to say that these events shook the very foundations of any (positivist) rationality and objectivity that are still expected from academic research. Unapologetically, it was impossible for us to maintain our academic integrity without forging intimate and lasting relationships with the respondents and their families beyond the field-work 'guidelines'. While we endeavoured to focus on children's media use, we often struggled to maintain our academic and human sanity facing the unfolding atrocities, and their direct and indirect implications on the research participants. The more we delved in, and bore witness to, the lives and minds of child respondents amid these volatile times, the harder it was for us to shake off the creeping angst over the grim prospects of Arab future generations that was unfolding before us.

Throughout the three years and until many more to come, we are as haunted by the sufferings involved in these encounters as humbled and disconcerted by our privilege as diasporic researchers operating from within the lofty protocols of academia (both in Western and Arab settings). As they stand, these bureaucratic protocols leave little room for a meaningful conversation around the symbiotic suffering and trauma shared by the researchers and research subjects beyond their ascribed research categories. In this volume, we thought it important to start this conversation, not with the intention to prioritise 'our' suffering over 'theirs', but in an effort to resuscitate the ethics of a shared humanity within and beyond the research process.

## THE BOOK

Chapter 2, 'The Poetics of Self-Reflexivity: Arab Diasporic Children in London and Media Uses', reflects on the methodological challenges we encountered in London (July–December 2013), conducting family observations and four workshops with young children of Arab origin between the ages of seven and twelve. London as a site of fieldwork hurled us into a complex, yet productive entanglement between ontology, ethics, and epistemology which we subsequently encountered, and in varied capacities, in Casablanca and Beirut. In the case of London, we were especially interested in the ways in which British children of Arab origin intentionally perform being-in-the-world by navigating through multiple forms of subjectification and cultural tastes. This, we argue, making use of Keightley and Pickering's concept, the 'mnemonic imagination' (2012), results into the production of what we term a 'mnemonic diasporic habitus', a fluid and performative interplay between different cultural times and repertoires. Chapter 2 also contextualises the politics of 'access and (mis)trust' within larger debates around othering, racism, and Islamophobia in the UK and engages reflexively with our *implicatedness* and entanglement as Arab diasporic ethnographers researching Arab diasporic children and their media uses in the UK. We analyse the complex ways in which the children use media technologies mnemonically and poetically to carve out an agential diasporic space.

Chapter 3, 'Ethnography as Double-Thrownness and the Face of the Sufferer as Media', provides a self-reflexive account of ethnographic research conducted in a Hezbollah-controlled area of Beirut close to the refugee camp, Burj Al-Brajneh, between July and August 2015. It focuses on the ethnographic fieldwork conducted with a Syrian refugee family including the mother, father, and five children. It engages with the family's uses of 'media' in the household through the un-concealment of the political economy of the fear that marks the family's everydayness. This chapter will show how both the researchers and the interlocutors were caught up in the political economy of fear produced by the context of war and the sectarian politics imposed by Hezbollah. The chapter rethinks the *whatness* of media, moving from a conventional definition of broadcasting/digitality/screen/computer to a more ontological and pluralistic interpretation that considers media as extended bodily forms of technicity. It argues that limiting the *worldliness* of the media to screen-media reinforces the power of the present absence: the structural mediation of power and ideology through the poster of the martyr—the religious leader—the poem on the wall—mural art—mourning women—the funeral—or what amounts to the aesthetics of structural violence. We show how the material realities and lived experiences of the Maimoun family as Syrian refugees in Beirut have altered our methodological course, as our roles oscillated between those of ethnographers and those of social workers. In this chapter, we make the case that our preoccupation with media and cultural analysis has alienated/detached us as scholars of media and cultural studies, from a key experiential moment: a philosophical pre-moment. In this chapter, we advance the following critique: in a world of chronic crises, we (scholars of media and cultural studies) have forgotten what it means to encounter suffering through the face of the sufferer. We seek refuge in Plato's cave again—not because of inability to tell the real from—shadowy reflections, but because the reflections (as mediatised experience) offer us—refuge, comfort, and distance. Our forgetfulness of suffering and the face of the sufferer have immersed us deep into a kind of 'sequestration' where language (academic language/language games/turf wars) takes precedence over experiencing a world in crisis. We have not forgotten about being-in-the-world, we have remorselessly turned philosophy on its head—philosophy has itself become a tool of sequestration—a shelter from the face of the sufferer. The faces of the sufferers, had made it possible for us to reconnect with what Levinas calls the *uniqueness* of the face of the other, the type of uniqueness that is being ceaselessly sequestrated by techno-televisual mediatisation. Encountering the face of the other, we argue in this chapter, is the *medium*. This chapter also introduces a key methodological concept, inspired by the work of Heidegger, which we call 'double-thrownness'. Our thrownness as ethnographers, we demonstrate in this chapter, was traversal and processual. We show how being thrown into the messiness of the field has a triangular and 'intra-active'[7] structure: double-thrownness is at once an ontological and an ethical (affective) condition as well as a thinking/figuring out process. It is the intersectional point or, to use Karen Barad's (2007) term, the kind of 'entanglement' where the ontological, ethical, and epistemological collide and interact (see also Sarah Nutall 2009).[8]

In Chapter 4, 'Networked World-Making: Children's Encounters with Media Use', we focused on children's everyday media use by departing from the double-focus of media and child-centric approaches. This departure was intended to connect children's media use with media objects through which they weave their world-making processes across layered material and phantasmagoric spatialities and temporalities. The chapter spots on the phenomenological understanding of world-making as part of a cultural encounter involving being-in-the-world. It reconciles it with actor-network theory that articulates 'being' as 'doing'. This compound theoretical elaboration allowed us to expand world-making as a process of being-doing that connects children to the media objects they use and the various discursive and affective networks that they engage with. Adopting a comparative approach to children's media use across the three sites of London, Casablanca, and Beirut, it brings forward key findings that speak of the contextual and cross-contextual intersections involved in these networks of mediation. Through this elaboration, the notion of *home* extends across the everyday spaces children occupy as well as the mediated temporalities brought not only by the media they use but also by the significant socio-cultural and political mediations powering children's cultural encounters with the adult worlds. The chapter also explores the relationship between children and media objects outside of the subject–object hierarchy. Instead, it connects actors and objects in a horizontal mapping of affectivity and intimacy. This exploration reveals the usefulness of attending to the value of objects as ethnographic elements in their own right, shifting focus from their accidental 'availability' to their 'presence' as mediators of children's world-making activities.

In Chapter 5, Children, Media as '*equipment*' and *Worldliness*, we take on two further Heideggerian concepts—*worldliness* and *equipment* and apply them, because of their relevance and usefulness, to our ethnographic research on children and the media in the Arab region. In this chapter, we are concerned with the 'intra-active' (see Barad 2007) structures that make up the children's world, their being-in, as the context through which we could make sense of their relationship to media. Fieldwork taught us to be patient. It taught us to put our institutionalised academic pursuits on hold. A cut needed to be made, a kind of de-mediatisation was necessary for us to observe other things, other phenomena that we later learnt were not disconnected from media uses, such as friendships, face, sounds, size of households, environment, habitus, and everyday talk, all of which can easily be ignored by a more media-centric approach. *Worldliness* presumes a distinctive structure in the way it un-conceals itself as such: the world. For Heidegger, phenomenology concerns itself by default with visible phenomena, with the world's 'availableness'. *Worldliness* in this case is conceived as a totality of objects that are visible to us. In borrowing the Heideggerian concept *worldliness*, we aim to explore *worldliness* as a totality in which media is a constituent in the everyday lives of the children with whom we worked. Our focus in this chapter is on the ways in which media technology and the communicative processes it instigates can, alongside other phenomena, shape children's ontological experience of being-in-the-world. This chapter is concerned with *worldliness* as outwardness that comes to the fore in its shared-ness. It is a being-in-the world *with*. It was this phenomenological positioning as a default position for thinking about children's media uses (an engagement with the children's worldliness and the role of the media as equipment in it) that revealed for us the hidden structures and phenomena over which the children have no power and are not of their making. So, in a sense, this chapter is a conversation with and against Heidegger's phenomenological approach. Here, we argue that a study of visible phenomena in and by itself fails to capture the complexity of worldliness and, in our case, children's worldliness. While the children use media texts not merely for purposes of gratification but also as equipment to carve out 'mnemonic'[9] extensions of self (see also Chapter 5) as well as agential extensions of cultural time and space, they do so within hidden and unequal structures that put them at a disadvantage at the level of creativity, education, and other public service rights as young citizens. So, this chapter is an attempt to both think with and against phenomenological approaches that intentionally avoid the question of power in their analyses.

## Notes

1. Bahrain, UAE, Qatar. These trade relations were suspended in 2009.
2. A study by Kovacic and Karamat (2005) reveals deep intra-regional disparities at the level of ICT use in terms of both the static relative difference and the time distance factor. Gulf countries showed a distinct lead in both variables, while internet use in some countries like Egypt and Lebanon fluctuated depending on the governmental policies for building infrastructure and popularising use across their populations.
3. In the same way, the same scholarship is fascinated with, and worried about, virtual reality and artificial intelligence today.
4. In the 2008 UNESCO report, surveying literature on children and the media in the Arab world (including more than 40 empirical case studies) dating from the 1970s till the late 1990s, Samy Tayie shows how most of the case studies are largely based on quantitative methods, focusing largely on television as a predominant medium of entertainment. http://milunesco.unaoc.org/children-and-mass-media-in-the-arab-world-a-second-level-analysis-2/.
5. The Israeli population includes 20% non-Jews. Commonly referred to as Arab Israelis, this group constitutes the remnants of the indigenous Palestinian populations who were ethnically cleansed from their lands by Jewish settlers paving the way to the establishment of the state of Israel in 1948.
6. All four alleged attackers were non-Arab; three of them were of Pakistani origin and the fourth was a convert of Jamaican origin.
7. "The neologism "intra-action" signifies the mutual constitution of entangled agencies. That is, in contrast to the usual "interaction," which assumes that there are separate individual agencies that precede their interaction, the notion of intra-action recognizes that distinct agencies do not precede, but rather emerge through, their intra-action. It is important to note that the "distinct" agencies are only distinct in a relational, not an absolute, sense, that is, agencies are only distinct in relation to their mutual entanglement; they don't exist as individual elements" (Barad 2007: 33).

8. In dealing with the concept 'entanglement', in a postcolonial context, Sarah Nuttall (2009) defines the term as: 'a condition of being twisted together or entwined, involved with; speaks of an intimacy gained, even if it was resisted, or ignored or uninvited. It is a term which may gesture towards as relationship that is complicated, ensnaring, in a tangle, but which also implies human foldedness' (2009: 1).

9. Our work on children's mnemonic imagination is inspired by Emily Keightley and Michael Pickering's work (2012) *The Mnemonic Imagination: Remembering as Creative Practice*, where they steer away from sociologically and psychologically deterministic interpretations of memory and advocate a focus on the relations between personal and popular memory and interplay between situated and mediated experience relationship. See also Chapter 5 where we engage with the concept of 'mnemonic diasporic habitus'.

## BIBLIOGRAPHY

Adorno, T., & Horkheimer, M. (1972 [1944]). The Culture Industry: Enlightenment as Mass Deception. In T. Adorno & M. Horkheimer (Eds.), *Dialectics of Enlightenment* (J. Cumming, Trans.). New York: Herder and Herder.

Alasuutari, P. (1999). Introduction: Three Phases of Reception Studies. In P. Alasuutari (Ed.), *Rethinking the Media Audience*. London: Sage.

al-Mesfer, M. (n.d.). Tahlil al-risala al-i'lamiya: Ta'thir al-fada'iyat al-'arabiyya 'ala alshabab al-'arabi [Analysis of the Media Message: The Effect of Arab Satellite Channels on Arab Youth]. *al-Mufakkir Journal, 3*, 31–61.

al-Salmi, L., & Smith, P. H. (2015). The Digital Biliteracies of Arab Immigrant Mothers. *Literacy Research: Theory, Method, and Practice, 64*, 193–209.

Amezaga Albizu, J. (2007). Geolinguistic Regions and Diasporas in the Age of Satellite Television. *International Communication Gazette, 69*(3), 239–261.

Ang, I. (1985). *Watching Dallas: Soap Opera and the Melodramatic Imagination*. London: Methuen.

Awan, F. (2016). *Occupied Childhoods: Discourses and Politics of Childhood and Their Place in Palestinian and Pan-Arab Screen Content for Children* (PhD thesis). University of Westminster.

Barad, K. (2007). *Meeting the Universe Halfway: Quantum Physics and the Entanglement of Matter and Meaning*. London: Duke University Press.

Bird, S. E. (2003). *The Audience in Everyday Life*. London: Routledge.

Buckingham, D. (Ed.). (2002). *Small Screens: Television for Children* (pp. 38–60). Leicester: Leicester University Press.

Buckingham, D. (2008). Children and Media: A Cultural Studies Approach. In S. Livingstone & K. Drotner (Eds.), *The International Handbook of Children, Media and Culture*. London: Sage.

Buckingham, D., & Bragg, S. (2004). *Young People, Sex and the Media: The Facts of Life*. London: Palgrave Macmillan.

Buckingham, D., & Sefton-Green, J. (1994). *Cultural Studies Goes to School: Reading and Teaching Popular Culture*. London: Taylor and Francis.

Buckingham, D., Davies, H., Jones, K., & Kelley, P. (1999). *Children's Television Britain: History, Discourse and Policy*. London: British Film Institute.

Buijzen, M., van der Molen, J. W., & Sondij, P. (2007). Parental Mediation of Children's Emotional Responses to a Violent News Event. *Communication Research, 34*(2), 212–230.

Chatterjee, P. (1993). *The Nation and Its Fragments: Colonial and Postcolonial Histories*. Princeton: Princeton University Press.

Critcher, C. (2008). Making Waves: Historical Aspects of Public Debates About Children and Mass Media. In S. Livingstone & K. Drtoner (Eds.), *International Handbook of Children, Media and Culture* (pp. 91–104). London: Sage.

Cunningham, H. (1995). *Children and Childhood in Western Society Since 1500*. London: Longman.

Dashty. (2010). Athar Mushahadat Al Baramij Al Fada'iya `ala Al Al Maharat Al Ijtima`iya lil Tofl Al Arabi [The Effects of Watching Satellite Channels on the Social Skills of the Arab Child].

Deacon, R., & Parker, B. (1995). Education as Subjection and Refusal: An Elaboration on Foucault. *Curriculum Studies, 3*(2), 109–122.

Dorsky, S., & Stevenson, B. T. (1995). Childhood and Education in Highland North Yemen. In E. Fenea (Ed.), *Children in the Muslim Middle East* (pp. 309–324). Austin: University of Text Press.

Drotner, K. (1999). Dangerous Media? Panic Discourses. *Paedogogica Historica, 35*(3), 593–619.

Fabian, J. (1983). *Time and the Other*. New York: Columbia University Press.

Foucault, M. (1978). Governmentality. In G. Burchell, C. Gordon, & P. Miller (Eds.), *The Foucault Effect: Studies in Governmentality* (pp. 87–104). London: Harvester Wheatsheaf.

Fuchs, C. (2016). *Critical Theory of Communication*. London: University of Westminster Press.

Fuchs, C. (2017). *Social Media: A Critical Introduction* (2nd ed.). London: Sage.

Gittins, D. (2009). The Historical Construction of Childhood. In M. J. Kehily (Ed.), *An Introduction to Childhood Studies* (2nd ed., pp. 35–49). Maidenhead, UK and New York: Open University Press.

Haboush, K. (2007). Working with Arab American Families: Culturally Competent Practice for School Psychologists. *Psychology in the Schools, 44*(2), 183–198.

Hendrick, H. (1997). Constructions and Reconstructions of British Childhood: An Interpretive Survey, 1800 to the Present. In A. James & A. Prout (Eds.), *Constructing and Reconstructing Childhood: Contemporary Issues in the Sociological Study of Childhood* (pp. 34–62). London: Falmer Press.

Heywood, C. (2001). *A History of Childhood: Children and Childhood in the West from Medieval to Modern Times.* Cambridge: Polity Press.

Jenks, C. (2009). Constructing Childhood Sociologically. In M. J. Kehily (Ed.), *An Introduction to Childhood Studies* (2nd ed., pp. 93–111). Maidenhead, UK and New York: Open University Press.

Keightley, E., & Pickering, M. (2012). *The Mnemonic Imagination: Remembering as Creative Practice.* London: Palgrave.

Kovacic, Z., & Karamat, P. (2005). An Alternative Measure of the Digital Divide Between Arab Countries. In *Proceedings of the Second International Conference on Innovations in Information Technology.* Dubai: United Arab Emirates University College of Information Technology.

Lazovsky, R. (2007). Educating Jewish and Arab Children for Tolerance and Coexistence in a Situation of Ongoing Conflict: An Encounter Program. *Cambridge Journal of Education, 37*(3), 391–408.

Lemish, D., & Pick-Alony, R. (2014). Inhabiting Two Worlds: The Role of News in the Lives of Jewish and Arab Children and Youth in Israel. *International Communication Gazette, 76*(2), 128–151.

Leurs, K. (2015). *Digital Passages: Migrant Youth 2.0: Diaspora, Gender and Youth Cultural Intersections.* Amsterdam: Amsterdam University Press.

Livingstone, S. (2002). *Young People and New Media.* London: Sage.

Mansour, N. (2018). Unmaking the Arab/Muslim Child: Lived Experiences of Media Use in Two Migratory Settings. *Middle East Journal of Culture and Communication, 11*(1), 91–110.

Marshall, J. D. (1989). Foucault and Education. *Australian Journal of Education, 33*(2), 99–113.

Mcluhan, M. (1994 [1964]). *Understanding Media: The Extensions of Man.* Cambridge: MIT Press.

Meer, N. (2007). Muslim Schools in Britain: Challenging Mobilisations or Logical Developments? *Asia Pacific Journal of Education, 27*(1), 55–71.

Messenger Davies, M. (2008). Studying Children's Television (Goodnight Mr. Tom). In G. Creeber (Ed.), *The Television Genre Book* (pp. 92–97). London: Palgrave Macmillan.

Moores, S. (1993). *Interpreting Audiences: The Ethnography of Media Consumption.* London: Sage.

Morley, D. (1980). *The Nationwide Audience.* London: British Film Institute.

Morley, D. (1986). *Family Television: Cultural Power and Domestic Leisure.* London: Comedia.

Morley, D. (1992). *Television Audiences and Cultural Studies.* London: Routledge.

Nuttall, Sarah. (2009). *Entanglement, Literary and Cultural Reflections on Post-Apartheid.* Johannesburg: Wits University Press.

Radway, J. (1984). *Reading the Romance: Women, Patriarchy, and Popular Literature.* Philadelphia: University of Pennsylvania Press.

Rinnawi, K. (2012). 'Instant Nationalism' and the 'Cyber Mufti': The Arab Diaspora in Europe and the Transnational Media. *Journal of Ethnic and Migration Studies, 38*(9), 1451–1467. https://doi.org/10.1080/13691 83x.2012.698215.

Rodman, G. (2004). *Media in a Changing World: History, Industry, Controversy.* New York: McGraw-Hill.

Sabry, T. (2007). An Interview with Paddy Scannell. *Westminster Papers in Communication and Culture, 4*(2), 3–23.

Sakr, Naomi. (2002). *Satellite Realms: Transnational Television, Globalisation and the Middle East.* London: I.B. Tauris.

Sakr, Naomi. (2007). *Arab Television Today.* London: I.B. Tauris.

Saloom, R. (2005). I Know You Are, but What Am I? Arab-American Experiences Through the Critical Race Theory Lens. *Hamline Journal of Public Law and Policy, 27*(1), 55–76.

Scannell, P. (2014). *Television and the Meaning of the Live: An Enquiry into the Human Situation.* Cambridge: Polity Press.

Scourfield, J., Gilliat-Ray, S., Khan, A., & Otri, S. (2013). *Muslim Childhood: Religious Nurture in a European Context.* Oxford: Oxford University Press.

Slone, M., Shechner, T., & Khoury, O. F. (2011). Parenting Style as a Moderator of Effects of Political Violence: Cross-Cultural Comparison of Israeli Jewish and Arab Children. *International Journal of Behavioral Development, 36*(1), 62–70.

Tayie, S. (2008). *Children and Mass Media in the Arab World: A Second Level Analysis UNESCO.* https://milunesco.unaoc.org/mil-articles/children-and-mass-media-in-the-arab-world-a-second-level-analysis-2/.

Weber, M. (2015). The Distribution of Power with the Gemeinschaft: Classes, *Stände,* Parties. In D. Waters & T. Waters (Eds. and Trans.). *Weber's Rationalism and Modern Society: New Translations on Politics, Bureaucracy and Social Stratification.* New York: Palgrave Macmillan.

Williams, R. (1989). *Resources of Hope: Culture, Democracy, Socialism.* London: Verso.

World Bank. (2017). *Staff Estimates Using the World Bank's Total Population and Age/Sex Distributions of the United Nations Population Division's World Population Prospects: 2017 Revision.* https://data.worldbank.org/indicator/SP.POP.0014.TO?locations=1A&year_high_desc=false.

FIELD NOTE

Creative Workshop 4, Casablanca, July 2014.

# CHAPTER 2

# The Poetics of Self-Reflexivity: Arab Diasporic Children in London and Media Uses

**Abstract** In this chapter, we reflect on the methodological challenges we encountered in London (September–December 2013), conducting family observations and four workshops with young children of Arab origin between the ages of seven and twelve. We contextualise the politics of 'access and (mis)trust' within larger debates around othering, racism, and Islamophobia in the UK and engage reflexively with our entanglement as Arab diasporic ethnographers researching Arab diasporic children and their media uses in the UK. Using notes from our ethnographic diaries and evidence from our participant observation, we examine the ways in which British children of Arab origin intentionally perform being-in-the-world by navigating through multiple forms of subjectification and cultural tastes. Interplay between different cultural temporalities and repertoires, we argue, produces and is operated through an agential, mnemonic diasporic habitus.

**Keywords** Mnemonic · Diaspora · Habitus · Performativity · Media uses · Mistrust · Islam · Children · Method

An earlier version of this chapter was published in Mansour, N., & Sabry, T. (2017). (Mis)trust, Access and the Poetics of Self-reflexivity: Arab Diasporic Children in London and Media Consumption. In N. Sakr & J. Steemers (Eds.), *Children's TV and Digital Media in the Arab World: Childhood, Screen Culture and Education* (pp. 207–226). London: I.B. Tauris. Used with permission from Bloomsbury Publishing Plc.

© The Author(s) 2019
T. Sabry and N. Mansour, *Children and Screen Media in Changing Arab Contexts*, https://doi.org/10.1007/978-3-030-04321-6_2

33

# INTRODUCTION

This chapter reflects on ethnographic research conducted in London (September–December 2013), involving family observations and four workshops with young children of Arab origin between the ages of 7 and 12. In the case of the London children, we were especially interested in the ways in which British children of Arab origin intentionally perform being-in-the-world by navigating through multiple forms of subjectification, cultural tastes, and temporalities. This, we argue, results in a mnemonic diasporic habitus.[1]

In this chapter, we reflect not so much on material from the participant observations and children's creative workshops, but on the methodological issues that emerged from fieldwork in the UK. The range of issues and challenges we faced in the field as two Arab diasporic ethnographers, researching Arab diasporic children living in London, triggered so much reflexive debate and discussion among the two researchers and the rest of the research team that we consider the methodological issues we faced important enough to form this chapter's main object of enquiry. These concerns resonate with methodological and ethical questions arising from research with London children from various ethnic backgrounds (for example, see Samantha 2002; James 2001; Zeitlyn and Mand 2012).

The methodological process of framing, planning, and conducting ethnography became a site for renegotiating the subjectivities of researcher and research subject. In our case, the 'field' of research moved from anthropology's conventional positioning as 'being "out there" practised by "other" people' and was discursively relocated within the researchers' and research subjects' 'home' (Zeitlyn and Mand 2012: 988). Thus, it contested the delineations of what is meant by Arab diaspora, how the diasporic researcher constructs herself or himself in relation to the diasporic subject, and the ways in which research subjects negotiate their participation in the research process.

This chapter discusses difficulties encountered by the ethnographers in recruiting participants for the research. It contextualises the politics of access and (mis)trust within larger debates around otherness, racism, and Islamophobia in the UK. It also engages, reflexively, with the politics of implicatedness on the part of Arab diasporic ethnographers researching Arab diasporic children. Engaging with 'doing-being self-reflexive as poetics', the chapter further discusses the politics of (mis)trust by showing how performing a mnemonic diasporic habitus (negotiation of memory and self in a diasporic context) extends Bourdieu's (1984) notion of habitus to include Butler's (1990) performativity. It is through the affective performing of habitus that a *third* mnemonic language of identification is created. Similar research on transnational childhoods (see Marcus 1995) notes that even when ethnography actually takes place in what is physically a single site, it still relates to what are effectively transnational constructions of childhood, experienced through the everydayness of home and exile. Throughout the ethnographic conversation, research subjects express their transnational selves by "evok[ing] multiple sites through an explicit reference to other sites which are 'off-stage' [...resulting in] strategically situated (single-site) ethnography" (Marcus 1995, quoted in Zeitlyn and Mand 2012: 989). This performance, we argue, is negotiated through and across parent cultures, the cultures of researchers as mediators and London's youth cultures.

The chapter analyses children's affective performances and narrativity while being aware that "[i]deas about children directly impinge upon the experience of childhood which children themselves have" (James 1993: 72). Hence, we sought to conduct reflexive research that involves deconstructing the dominant notions of childhood and explicating the power relations inherent in the relationship between researchers, parents, and children. It rehearses how a 'mnemonic diasporic habitus' may be a useful tool for unpacking the politics of diasporic identities.

## Framing Problems of Access and (Mis)Trust

Having access to and establishing a relationship of trust with children and their families are, as ethnographic processes, rarely contextualised within the socio-cultural environments and the material realities by which they are determined. In preparation for our ethnographic research in London, we had to locate four families of Arab origin for the purpose of conducting home ethnography and 24 children of Arab origin for the purpose of conducting four separate workshops.

As researchers residing in London for over two decades, we have been part of the changing public discourses on the UK's Arab diaspora. We both came to London individually without any links to diasporic Arab communities. The compound and fluid selving process gradually blended the migrant narrative with increasing daily involvement with the UK as a final destination country. Over time, we both have joined the many Londoners who juggle with a native cultural repertoire, and a British lived experience. Thus, questions like "where are you from?" have become harder to answer. Our social networks did not rely on our respective diasporic groups and we both were at the margins of the intra-diasporic subjectification dynamics in London.

Engaging in the London fieldwork necessitated an active performative process to connect with the Arab diaspora and to reposition ourselves as insiders to the Arab community. This process required engaging with the stratifying techniques of belonging and otherness with our native communities that we are culturally familiar with but effectively knew little about.

With no prior connection to the Arab diaspora in London, it was not possible to rely on personal contacts to recruit child respondents. The prominent physicality of diasporic communities within the geography of London made it an obvious choice to initiate access. Our aim was to find entry points linking us to the varied loci of Arab communities rather than going through elitist and structured channels of Arab cultural educational production in London (including private schools and cultural institutions funded by Arab embassies). While these channels are conventionally used in children's research because of their potential easy access, they remain laden with power dynamics that could hinder children's ability to opt out and their willingness to express themselves freely (Olwig and Gulløv 2003).

Our strategy was to target enclaves in London, including schools, known to have a predominant or at least a significant Arab diasporic population. So, we targeted places like Ladbroke Grove and Shepherds Bush, known to have a sizeable Moroccan population, and Marble Arch, Kilburn and Edgware Road, known to attract a largely Middle Eastern population (Iraq, Lebanon, Egypt, etc.). We had designed a leaflet written both in Arabic and in English explaining the purpose of the research and the source of funding. To focus our energies, we then opted to target our native Arab diasporic communities with whom we as researchers share a common culture and a structure of feeling. Hence, we each targeted localities in London that had a significant Lebanese and Moroccan population and leafleted in the street, cafés, supermarkets, and grocery shops. After six weeks of trying, it was the religious communities of these two groups—a mosque in Ladbroke Grove and a church in Swiss Cottage—that allowed us access to workshop participants. However, agreeing to give us access to children in these communities was followed by another eight-week period during which we, as researchers, were coaxingly and politely interrogated again and again about the nature and objectives of the research. We were only let in after literally dozens of email exchanges and a number of one-to-one meetings with community leaders in these religious establishments.

Negotiating access threw us into the contextual intra dynamics of our respective communities, involving mainly tapping into our existing commercial networks such as grocers and butchers in the area. Nisrine's interaction with Lebanese shopkeepers in Kilburn is an example of the complex intra-politics of diasporic relations, the insider–outsider researcher and migrant positionality, and the continuous crossing over, rearticulating and blurring lines between 'us' and 'them' (Marcus 1995). With every visit, shopkeepers tested the insider–outsider positionality in relation to the many facets of the intra-Lebanese habitus that revolve around the religion of birth. Through Lebanon's recent history of civil war (1975–1990) and until today, religion of birth remains a marker for intra-Lebanese differences. It is a compulsory legal political category enshrined in the civic records of every Lebanese citizen regardless of their personal beliefs. These queries occurred smoothly, in indirect ways reflecting the contextual importance of negotiating access. A seemingly basic question like 'where are you from?' unfolds a powerful categorising subtext that ties geography with religion, since the Lebanese civil war resulted in a geographic segregation of population on the basis of religion of birth. When birthplace, and hence religion of birth, matched those of the shopkeeper in question, it was a first step into establishing an initial insider rapport, tracing connections back to Lebanon and the Lebanese diaspora in London. However, religion of birth is only a partial marker of the intra-Lebanese diasporic habitus. Further queries aimed to discern the researcher's links with social and religious institutions and practices within the Shi`a community in London. When the researcher could not show prior involvement with members of the community, key contacts like shopkeepers restricted access to the Lebanese Shi`a diasporic community.

In contrast, the researcher's lack of identification with a specific Shi`a diasporic habitus guaranteed access to the Christian community through the Lebanese Maronite church in London. The priest, who was the main authority in the church, went through the same geographic categorising exercise to probe the researcher's birthplace, noting the researcher's religious 'otherness'. However, more probing revealed the researcher's individual migration trajectory, lack of religious involvement with the Shiʻa community in London, and professional occupation. For the priest, these attributes were markers of a 'civilised other' reflected in his comments such as 'Wow you are well educated. Nowadays the Shiʻa community in Lebanon has evolved'. Hence, an invitation to become an insider was extended to visit the church and engage with the religious rituals, as 'the church is open for all Lebanese regardless of their religious affiliation'. Effectively, performing the friendly Other through attending the Sunday Mass turned out to be the main channel for recruiting Lebanese respondents.

While we have no doubt that the difficulties we experienced in recruiting participants were largely due to the ethical sensitivities implicated in researching children (in relation to the protection and well-being of minors as research participants), we also attribute them to socio-cultural and political variables. These include interpretations of domesticity as a private space, Arabophobia/Islamophobia, and gender roles. Since the terrorist attacks of 9/11 in New York and 7/7 in London, there has been a conspicuous and ceaseless coverage of Islam and Muslims in British mainstream media. Such coverage tends to, on the whole, discursively lump Islam, Muslims, Islamism, and terrorism together as though these were inseparable categories. Over time, this has created a great sense of suspicion (and hatred in the case of far-right groups and many of their members who come largely from disgruntled poor working classes) towards Muslim and Arab communities in the UK (Matar 2006). Islamophobia is the result of an intersection between the encoding and the decoding of racist representations of Muslims and Arabs as others. What is seldom studied or researched is first: how a systematic use of negative coverage about Islam and Muslims has affected or is affecting British Muslim identities and their conceptions of otherness; and secondly: what implications this has for access to ethnographic research with Muslim and Arab communities in the UK (Bolognani 2007; Sundas 2008; Scourfield et al. 2013). We are of the view that the challenge we faced as researchers in getting access to Arab families' homes is largely due to a suspicion that Arab communities have themselves developed towards British media and the establishment they represent. We were denied access (mistrusted) because we were seen, regardless of our apparent traces of Arabness, as part of a racist system. Our research focus on London children of Arab origin and their media worlds may well have been misread by the parents as a sneaky attempt on our part (since we represent the system) to spy on Muslim/Arab children (catch them early on). Questions such as 'why looking at Arab kids?', 'what do you want to know?', 'who is funding this research?' reflected a deep-seated anxiety related to the growing Islamophobic climate in the UK. One of the parents, with whom we conducted home observations on and off over eight weeks, jokingly remarked in the last family visit that we 'could be spies after all'.

Our constant insider–outsider repositioning was tested in our role as researchers investigating intra-diasporic research on Arab children and the media. The nature of the inquiry necessitates carrying out home visits over a three-week time span. Through our contacts, a sense of anxiety and suspicion emerged as to the purpose of the research project. Muslim contacts were the most reluctant to participate in the research, in contrast to Christian contacts who were little concerned with the underlying motives of the research. In this instance, our positioning as intra-diasporic researchers was embedded with a sense of paranoia from some contacts, suspecting that we were potentially acting as double agents, delving into the intimate lives of our 'own' communities and reporting back to the British system, since the funding was granted by the AHRC.

The problem of access and mistrust is the product of a relational structure and has to be understood in a wider conjunction with factors such as the gender of the researcher (Tarik is male and Nisrine is female) and discourses of domesticity. We felt that our genders as researchers were unquestionably implicated not only in problems of access, but also in power relations between the researcher and the researched or the observer and the observed. Being a male ethnographer with an intention to observe children and families in homes brought two challenges. First, there is a general bias against males working with children due to the recent explosion of highly mediatised legal cases of paedophilia involving famous children's programmes presenters, educators, and other males engaging in direct professional contact with children. Second, some families found it culturally inappropriate to allow a male researcher into their homes when the male heads of the household are absent. Whether due to a traditional, patriarchal form of domesticity (perhaps with roots in religious discourse) or to the general gender bias discussed above, some mothers of participants felt more at ease conversing with and being observed by a female rather than a male researcher. Being a male researcher meant that Tarik could not attend all the family observations on his own. Indeed, a mixed gender team proved quite effective in diffusing these gender-related obstacles. Researching children of any origin is usually fraught with ethical implications and thus problems of access and trust are certainly not limited to our targeted group. However, we believe, it is reasonable to argue that, in the case of Arab and Muslim children living in London, problems of access and trust are further complicated by an increasingly privatised media sphere where representations of Arabness and Islam are still deeply rooted in an orientalist discourse. Similarly, entry into private spaces is problematic regardless of the participants' origin. Researchers remain relative strangers and entry into private spaces, regardless of geography or culture, will always be challenging.

Being a woman facilitated access to children due to the conventional gender caring roles associated with women. However, it also involved a process of negotiating gender performativity in relation to the dominant socio-cultural discourses on gender within the Arab diasporic communities. Various Lebanese contacts within the Lebanese diaspora in London found that being a single Lebanese woman with no family ties in London presents a set of non-conforming social practices. These gendered moralities hold the potential to position the female researcher at the margins of the diaspora's dominant gender norms. For instance, one contact person interpreted a non-conforming marital status as a sign of sexual availability and licence for sexual harassment. However, the overwhelming majority of contact persons accepted the researcher's different ways of life as a marker for a 'friendly outsider' and sought to maintain friendship ties after the end of the fieldwork.

## DOING 'BEING SELF-REFLEXIVE' AS POETICS: MNEMONIC DIASPORIC HABITUS BETWEEN PERFORMANCE AND AFFECT

Once in the field and in the homes of the families we observed, we were extremely conscious of the important task of building a rapport of trust with the children and their parents. While power relations between adult researchers and young respondents are part and parcel of research methodologies (Christensen and James 2000), we wanted our encounters with the families to mimic structures of ordinary everyday talk in an attempt to destabilise binaries between researcher and researched and produce textured types of knowledge beyond ageist, ethnic, and socio-cultural biases. We cannot say with certainty to what extent what was said and how the families behaved was totally free or untainted by relations of power or by the simple fact that we were 'strangers', but we certainly shared intimate moments with the families we observed, which involved dancing, singing, and telling jokes.

A three-way relationship between the diasporic researcher, parents, and children developed within the performative site of the home, detailed in Chapter 4. Initially, parents displayed tacit mistrust as they intently sat around the first few meetings with the kids. Gradually, they loosened their involvement, yet they remained omnipresent as silent and seemingly distracted observers. In most instances, parents were first-generation immigrants, attached to the cultural practices of their country of birth. They also avidly engaged with Arabic-speaking global satellite TV channels on a daily basis, a finding resonating with existing research on Arab diasporas in Europe (Harb and Bessaiso 2006; Matar 2006; Miladi 2006; Stolcke 1995). They spoke limited English and mingled primarily and almost exclusively with fellow diaspora members. We related to parents through tracing commonalities in our diasporic trajectories, an issue that children did not closely relate to. We exchanged narratives about our migration history, our legal status, and our perceptions of life in Lebanon/Morocco and the UK. The researchers' diasporic performativity with parents revolved around narratives of nostalgic belonging, manifested in affinity over food, pop culture, childhood experiences, and current anxiety in relation to the political insecurity wrapping the Arab region.

The mnemonic diasporic habitus was further expanded by our presence. Our performativity relied on making sense of and navigating through these overlapping cultural layers when relating to children and parents. Thus, we brought our own diasporic cultural repertoire into the dynamics, opening doors to exploration of the selving process. In many instances, we were positioned at the edge of the insider–outsider mnemonic diasporic boundaries. For example, children of Moroccan origin were curious about Nisrine's age and marital status and noted her short haircut as a novelty for an Arab woman (see Chapter 5). Lebanese children expressed a pronounced notion of sectarian and ethnic differences and considered Tarik different because of his darker complexion. We were able to relate to children through London-focused cultural practices, an area with which the parents struggled. For instance, our conversations covered popular audio-visual culture, articulations of London's urban youth culture, and contemplations on beliefs, hopes, and worries.

However, in listening to the children talk about their friends, family members, schools, and media worlds, often in the presence of their parents, we sensed early on that the telling of life stories/life worlds/ the unfolding narratives of self were mnemonically performed for us in a way that produced a discursive language we had to unpack semiotically. This language we later attributed to the workings of a mnemonic diasporic habitus, manifested in a dialectical relationship between different narratives of self and contextual environment (in our case, parent culture and the researchers' culture). We found it useful in our grappling with the children's performed narrativity to distinguish between 'habitus' as the sum of accumulated socio-cultural attributes and as an affectively performed habitus using mnemonic imagination. This allowed for navigation and negotiation of self between past and present, and between parent cultures, the culture of the researchers as Arabs, and London cultural context (detailed in Chapter 5). It is through the mnemonic imagination and the affective performance of diasporic habitus that a third discursive language about self is created.

What we are describing here, as 'a mnemonic diasporic habitus' is the result of our implicatedness in the research and in the lives of the children whom we were observing. As such, making sense of this type of habitus is for us not merely a matter of cultural interpretation, but also an object of methodological reflection, for the two things are inextricably linked. Our theoretical pursuit in unpacking the structures of a 'mnemonic diasporic habitus' is inspired by Emily Keightley and Michael Pickering's work (2012) *The Mnemonic Imagination: Remembering as Creative Practice,* where they steer away from sociologically and psychologically deterministic interpretations of memory and advocate a focus on the relations between personal and popular memory and interplay between situated and mediated experience (Keightley and Pickering 2012). The authors argue that the mnemonic imagination is key to these relations and this interplay, because it facilitates 'the transactional movement necessary for their co-existence' (Keightley and Pickering 2012). Here, the redrafting of memories of our past experience is not a fixed process. Experience in this case is ceaselessly traversing a temporalised space between the remembering subject and the changing intervening social forces with which it enters a dialectical relationship. In the case of our research with children from the Arab diaspora in London, the 'traversing of temporalised space' is a perpetual performance of selfhood, oscillating between an 'unlived' spatio-temporality, mnemonically performed by the parents for the children, which enters into dialogue with the children's 'lived' experience and their implicatedness in 'Londonness' not only as a spatio-symbolic space, but also as futuralness (Heidegger 2011: 80)[2] where children mnemonically imagine different ways of being in the world. Our role as ethnographers in this dialectical type of diasporic traversing was to facilitate the children's mnemonic imagination, to nurture it, and to encourage the parents to overcome their gatekeeping instincts and become aware of the imaginative work their children were doing.

Staying clear of modernist and deterministic interpretations of 'experience', Keightley and Pickering define experience as 'never exclusively personal or public, interiorised or outwardly facing, self-directed or the blind product of social forces', but always in flux and crossing between 'these mutually, informing categories' (Keightley and Pickering 2012: 19). The traversal movement of experience is predicated on a dual temporal structure, 'characterised by its continual unfolding in time while also acting back on the continuing development across time' (Keightley and Pickering 2012: 24). This dual structure allows the modern subject to creatively reflect 'narratively' about self across time. It is because of our access to *Erfahrung* (Keightley and Pickering 2012: 26) (the point where accumulated experience is evaluated) that our knowledge about self is crystallised. For the London children, accumulated experience is crystallised in a mnemonic, third discursive, and performative space. In other words, while accumulated experience may shape their identities, it is through their intentional and performative narrative of self, which they negotiate between memory and imagination, that their subject-hood comes to light.

Taking their cue from Dilthey's work on *Poetry and Experience*, Kant's distinction between reproductive (*re-collective*) and productive (*inventive*) imagination, and Marleau Ponty's situating of the 'real' and the 'unreal' within a dialectical relationship, Keightley and Pickering build a strong case against 'the deleterious consequences of analytical separation of memory and imagination'. Their concept, 'mnemonic imagination', moves beyond this tendency, insisting instead on a 'continuous interpenetration' of memory and imagination (Keightley and Pickering 2012: 76).

As we began to understand how habitus was performed for us through different affective strategies, we became conscious that we as ethnographers needed to modify our engagement, moving from being mere interviewers to performing being audiences. By 'poetics', we mean the mnemonic performativity that the children used to dialectically navigate through and between individual agents (habitus) and environment (field) to create a third meaning of self that lies at an intersection between the past, the present, and the future, but which strategically embodies and champions the present and the future over the past. A 12-year-old female participant, who was talking to us about her favourite music, showed us parts of a music video where a young female US pop singer is almost naked. The participant mimed the lyrics she knew by heart as she gazed at the pop star with admiration, then shyly glanced at her mother and us and complained about the pop star's decadent and debauched behaviour. The child displayed a range of subtle expressions in relation to explicit pop culture that could be picked up by researchers through the process of 'interpretive poetics [...] whereby layers of meaning in narrative texts are interrogated and interpreted in a way that mirrors a sophisticated reading of a poem' of which 'languages of the unsayables and woven and torn signifiers' are key interpretation registers (Rogers et al. 2005: 160).

However, children evoked their Arab past when intentionally invited by parents. Experiences and practices across temporality and geography were manifested in the diasporic habitus through the parents' media capital. Lebanese kids were exposed to Lebanese- and Arabic-speaking TV since it was the parents' default viewing choice. Lebanese parents also actively encouraged them to watch specific Lebanese TV shows ranging from comedy, to talk shows and sometimes, news. Children eagerly followed these shows, recounting the content to us. Similarly, they had regular contact with their relatives in Lebanon through online apps like Skype, Viber, and WhatsApp. Sometimes these relatives featured as part of their closest contacts.

Children located the Arab past within mnemonic recollections of a nostalgic heritage rather than an articulation of the present physicality of Lebanon/Morocco in relation to London. For instance, children of Lebanese origin were not able to place Lebanon on the world map, and were not aware of the precarious security situation there. However, the physicality of London was pronounced in their articulation of their daily lives. Their native language was English, with only little understanding of Arabic. Their friends were primarily Lebanese, in contrast to children of Moroccan origin who socialised regularly with various ethnicities. Their choice of music also reflected London's urban and pop culture.

Their Arabic music playlists were limited, featuring some patriotic and pop tracks. However, their English-speaking playlists were much longer and, regardless of their religiosity, they were up to date with the most explicit music video clips of artists such as Miley Cyrus and Rihanna.

This mnemonic past was projected into the future in varying ways. Children from Lebanese origin, who had never been to Lebanon, referred to their parents' country of origin in romantic terms of a home-land and exile that are far removed from their existence in London. Their accounts focused on the beauty of their village, and their hope to go back to the big house, pets, and garden they own there, contrasting it with their compact accommodation in Shepherds Bush. Children of Moroccan origin meanwhile evoked images of exoticism reminiscent of an ideal holiday destination. They talked at length of the good times they have in Morocco, especially recounting the food, the music, the sun, the sea, as well as the friendly relatives.

## Technologies of Self and Children's Media Worlds

We initially designed the rationale with a clear set of objectives at the heart of which lay a key focus on Arab children's reading and engagement with media texts broadcast by pan-Arab satellite channels. No sooner had we entered the field than we were challenged to rethink, not only our audience research questions (for UK children), but also our assumptions about the 'what' and 'how' of media uses among children of Arab origin in the UK. The research in London revealed a key finding: British children of Arab origin spoke little if no Arabic and preferred watching British-produced children programming over the pan-Arab satellite channels that their parents watched. This finding helped us to rethink our media focus, and the design of media diaries in ways that allowed the children to crea-tively map out their social and media worlds for us.

As a consequence, our starting point for researching the children's media use had shifted, from an idea in the ethnographer's head about what media were to how the children thought them and used them. Methodologically, this was a turning point in our engagement with phe-nomenology as an approach for studying the relationship between chil-dren and the media (see Chapters 3 and 4). As we embarked on the family observations, it became clear to us that the children's media uses relied on multiple devices (mobiles and tablets) and media (video games, music, and social media). In this sense, the practices of Londoner children of

Arab origin coincided with findings from EU-wide research that found children using media in individual and private spaces like their bedrooms and their mobile devices (Livingstone 2007; Livingstone et al. 2014). As we became more involved with family observations, we reworked our participant observation methods to allow for a freer and a more reflexive account of the children's narratives about self and media-cultures. Children used different media platforms (online and off line) not only strategically, but also intra-actionally (Barad 2007), as technologies of self through embodiment, where media become 'cultural frames' (Bird 2003: 3) and act as extensions of a 'mnemonic habitus' (see Mansour and Sabry 2017). The children wove narratives of subject-hood through identification with and in relation to media characters, sounds, and visuals. This type of narrativity was further helped by designing an experimental media diary, through which we attempted to explore not only the children's everyday media use but also how what they consume was used to operationalise their mnemonic diasporic habitus, giving us an insight into their media and social worlds. The diaries were a creative tool to get around the rigid communication dynamics that might ensue between researchers and children. Increasingly, diaries proved to be a particularly useful and versatile tool complementing ethnographic research (Hyers et al. 2006). The diaries had the merit of repositioning children as researchers engaged in recording and reflecting upon their own diasporic and media worlds. It also combined both qualitative and quantitative entries, allowing children to document their media use at the end of each day, in addition to reflecting on their diasporic and mnemonic habitus.

Using the diaries as a starting point for discussion, our line of inquiry during family observations followed a fluid, semi-structured (sometimes unstructured) approach where the children felt comfortable enough to move from one subject to another. In most cases, we only interfered to stimulate further talk. In one instance, a seven-year old danced for us, performed a rap song, and switched minutes later to telling us about a family member whom we were told was 'possessed'. As the discussion went on, this time including the father and a sister, the talk fluidly drifted to assertions about major pop stars like Madonna and Michael Jackson being Satan worshippers and part of a global conspiracy by the Illuminati secret society. Rather than seeing this as an incoherent form of narrativity, we picked on its theme/performance (pop culture, healing practices, and religious persecution) as a stimulus for further insight into the workings of a mnemonic diasporic habitus (see Chapter 4). What might appear on the surface, as a non-linear, fragmentary and therefore incoherent narrative of self, can under scrutiny be extremely useful in unpacking the constituent elements of a performed mnemonic, diasporic habitus.

We extended the flexible design of the media diary (which was intended to encourage talk about self) to the tasks we devised for the workshops, one of which was asking the children to work in groups as media producers to create a new Arab satellite channel targeting young Arabs living in the Arab region and in the diaspora. The task included designing a one-week running schedule for the new channel. Methodologically, our objective of simulating this task was to further explore the children's media uses and preferences. Since media use is deeply implicated in habitus, we also wanted to investigate the choices, modalities, and socio-cultural attitudes/values informing their production choices, negotiative processes, and decision-making. We were keen to understand how and whether the children's choice of programming informed their mnemonic habitus structures. For example, even though workshop participants were recruited through religious cultural centres, none of the hypothetical new satellite channels had any programming remotely close to a religious theme. Was this because the parents were not present? Might the children have negotiated a different set of programmes had the parents been present at the workshops? Although we do not intend to analyse ethnographic material in this chapter (for our focus here is purely on method), we want to emphasise how creative audience research approaches can delineate self-reflexive spaces that allow for a closer and a deeper insight, less into what we the researchers think about the world than into how the researched subjects experience the world. What we were keen to learn was how the children, as active audiences, understood, spoke about and mnemonically imagined their habitus in relation to their everyday media uses.

## Conclusion

Audience research rarely reflects on the intricacies and challenges posed by the designed research methods. Findings are always privileged as an end, even if they are always inextricably linked to the rationalising processes that come with method design. In our case it was clearly the methods and how we used them that shaped our conceptual framework, not vice versa. It was the reworking of the method that expanded the object of our enquiry and altered our interviewing techniques. Our method and conceptual framework entered a dialectical relationship. For example, as we began to grapple with the mnemonic diasporic habitus and its constituent elements (parent culture, London culture, and a third performative language), we intentionally varied our approach to participant observation to further probe and test our grappling with a type of habitus where, like Bhabha's (1994) 'third space', identities are always in flux, navigating and negotiating meaning through an ambivalent space of enunciation. Once we realised that children's identities were intentionally and affectively performed for us through 'everyday talk' (Dover 2007), dance, and music, we strategically moved towards a more phenomenological and a far less structured approach. We became, as Bird (2003: 3) would have put it, 'opportunist ethnographers.

## NOTES

1. This concept is further explained in the chapter using evidence from ethnography. Unlike the Bourdieusian conceptualisation of *habitus* which was critiqued for its ahistorical disregard for mobility and social change (see Garnham and Williams 1980: 222), we use the concept *mnemonic habitus* to delineate agency, change, and movement. Anthony King summarises this critique rather well, where he observed (2000) 'If the habitus were determined by objective conditions, ensuring appropriate action for the social position in which any individual was situated, and the habitus were unconsciously internalised dispositions and categories, then social change would be impossible. Individuals would act according to the objective structural conditions in which they found themselves, and they would consequently simply reproduce those objective conditions by repeating the same practices...new situations could never arise, nor could the habitus allow any transformation in practice (p. 247). Evidence emerging out of our ethnographic research with British children of Arab origin in London further substantiates the above critique. The children we worked with were able to navigate mnemonically between different cultural repertoires, helping them in the process to negotiate new strategies of self. Rather than simply repeating or reproducing socio-cultural practices determined a priori, the children were able to performatively, and discursively create movement within their own diasporic habitus and allowing for what King calls 'mutability' (2000: 427) in *habitus*. What determines the British-Arab children's habitus is not merely its objective constituents or elements, but the

mnemonic, strategic, and, let us add, the performative way, in which movement takes place within these constituents so as to create mutability.
3. Heidegger's *Zukünftigsein*, the state of readying oneself to 'receive the right impetus from the past in order to open it up'.

## BIBLIOGRAPHY

Barad, K. (2007). *Meeting the Universe Halfway: Quantum Physics and the Entanglement of Matter and Meaning*. London: Duke University Press.
Bhabha, H. (1994). *The Location of Culture*. Abingdon: Routledge.
Bird, E. (2003). *The Audience in Everyday Life: Living in a Media World*. Abingdon: Routledge.
Bolognani, M. (2007). Islam, Ethnography and Politics: Methodological Issues in Researching Amongst West Yorkshire Pakistanis. *International Journal of Social Research Methodology, 10*(4), 279–293.
Bourdieu, P. (1984). *Distinction: A Social Critique of the Judgment of Taste*. London: Routledge.
Butler, J. (1990). *Gender Trouble: Feminism and the Subversion of Identity*. New York: Routledge.
Christensen, P., & J, Allison (Eds.). (2000). *Research with Children: Perspectives and Practices*. London: Falmer Press.
Dover, C. (2007). Everyday Talk: Investigating Media Uses and Identity Amongst School Children. *Particip@tions, 4*(1).
Garnham, N., & Williams, R. (1980). Pierre Bourdieu and the Sociology of Culture: An Introduction. *Media, Culture and Society, 2*(3), 209–223.
Harb, Z., & Bessaiso, E. (2006). British Arab Muslim Audiences and Television After September 11. *Journal of Ethnic and Migration Studies, 32*(6), 1063–1076.
Heidegger, M. (2011). *The Concept of Time: The First Draft of Being and Time* [I. Farin, Trans.]. London: Bloomsbury Academic.
Hyers, L., Swim, J., & Mallet, R. (2006). The Personal Is Political: Using Daily Diaries to Examine Everyday Prejudice-Related Experiences. In S. Hesse-Biber & P. Leavy (Eds.), *Emergent Methods in Social Research* (pp. 313–336). London: Sage.
James, A. (1993). *Childhood Identities. Self and Social Relationships in the Experience of the Child*. Edinburgh: Edinburgh University Press.
James, A. (2001). Ethnography in the Study of Children and Childhood. In P. Atkinson, A. Coffey, S. Delamont, J. Lofland, & I. Lofland (Eds.), *Handbook of Ethnography* (pp. 246–257). London: Sage.
Keightley, E., & Pickering, M. (2012). *The Mnemonic Imagination: Remembering as Creative Practice*. Basingstoke: Palgrave Macmillan.
King, A. (2000). Thinking with Bourdieu Against Bourdieu: A Practical Critique of the Habitus. *Sociological Theory, 18*(3), 417–433.

Livingstone, S. (2007). From Family Television to Bedroom Culture: Young People's Media at Home. In E. Devereux (Ed.), *Media Studies: Key Issues and Debates* (pp. 302–321). London: Sage.

Livingstone, S., Haddon, L., Vincent, J., Kjartan, G., & Mascheroni, Ó. (2014). *Net Children Go Mobile: The UK Report*. London: London School of Economics and Political Science.

Mansour, N., & Sabry, T. (2017). (Mis)trust, Access and the Poetics of Self-Reflexivity: Arab Diasporic Children in London and Media Consumption. In N. Sakr & J. Steemers (Eds.), *Children's Tv and Digital Media in the Arab World: Childhood, Screen Culture and Education* (pp. 207–226). London: I.B. Tauris.

Marcus, G. (1995). Ethnography in/of the World System: The Emergence of Multi-Sited Ethnography. *Annual Review of Anthropology, 24,* 95–117.

Matar, D. (2006). Diverse Diasporas, One Meta-Narrative: Palestinians in the UK Talking About 11 September 2001. *Journal of Ethnic and Migration Studies, 32*(6), 1027–1040.

Miladi, N. (2006). Satellite Television News and the Arab Diaspora in Britain: Comparing Al-Jazeera, the BBC and CNN. *Journal of Ethnic and Migration Studies, 32*(6), 947–960.

Olwig, K. F., & Gulløv, E. (2003). Towards an Anthropology of Children and Place. In K. F. Olwig & E. Gulløv (Eds.), *Children's Places, Cross-Cultural Perspectives* (pp. 1–22). London: Routledge.

Punch, S. (2002). Research with Children: The Same or Different from Research with Adults?. *Childhood, 9*(3), 321–341.

Rinnawi, K. (2012). 'Instant Nationalism' and the 'Cyber mufti': The Arab Diaspora in Europe and the Transnational Media. *Journal of Ethnic and Migration Studies, 38*(9), 1451–1467.

Rogers, A., Casey, M., Ekert, J., & Holland, J. (2005). Interviewing Children Using an Interpretive Poetics. In S. Greene & D. Hogan (Eds), *Researching Children's Experience: Approaches and Methods* (p. 160). London: Sage.

Scourfield, J., Gilliat-Ray, S., Otri, S., & Khan, A. (2013). *Muslim Childhood: Religious Nurture in a European Context*. Oxford: Oxford University Press.

Stolcke, V. (1995). Talking Culture: New Boundaries, New Rhetoric of Exclusion in Europe. *Current Anthropology, 36*(3), 1–13.

Sundas, A. (2008). *Second and Third Generation Muslims in Britain: A Socially Excluded Group?* Identities, Integration and Community Cohesion (Oxford). http://www.portmir.org.uk/assets/pdfs/second-and-third-generation-muslims-in-britain-a-socially-excluded-group.pdf.

Zeitlyn, B., & Mand, K. (2012). Researching Transnational Childhoods. *Journal of Ethnic and Migration Studies, 38*(6), 987–1006.

# CHAPTER 3

# Ethnography as Double-Thrownness: War and the Face of the Sufferer as Media

**Abstract** This chapter provides a self-reflexive account of ethnographic research conducted in a Hezbollah-controlled area of Beirut close to the refugee camp, *Burj Al-Brajneh*. It engages with a Syrian refugee family's uses of 'media' in the household through the unpacking of the political economy of the fear that marks the family's everydayness. It will especially focus on the ways in which the ethnographers and the interlocutors were caught up in the context of war and the sectarian politics imposed by Hezbollah. Rethinking the *whatness* of media, this chapter argues that limiting the *worldliness* of the media to screen-media reinforces the power of the present absence. This chapter also introduces a new methodological concept, inspired by the work of Heidegger, which we call 'double-thrownness'. We show how our 'thrownness' as ethnographers was both traversal and processual. We show how our ethnographic experience in the South of Beirut was implicated in an entanglement where the ontological, ethical, and epistemological collide and interact.

**Keywords** Thrownness · Heidegger · War · Sectarianism · Face · Ethnography · Entanglement · Ethics · Media

## Introduction

Our entry into the field in Beirut was marked by a number of political events with which our ethnographic experience became entangled. The Lebanese did not have a president for over a year (2014–2015); the Lebanese people were out demonstrating on a regular basis, denouncing their government's corruption and incompetence in dealing with public service issues. Because of political squabbles between government agencies and private players, rubbish had not been collected for weeks, turning Beirut into a big stink (Thus, the demonstrators' slogan addressed to the Lebanese government: "YOU STINK"); the war in Syria had shown no signs of abating, with Hezbollah forces being openly and deeply involved in their support of the Assad regime. Syrian refugees kept crossing into Lebanon for fear of their lives, but were met by abject living conditions, no schooling for their children and had been suffering from racism and alienation. ISIS was around the corner and were, to many of the Lebanese we talked to, a source of threat and anxiety. It was within this charged political atmosphere that we embarked, in August 2015, on our ethnographic research in Beirut. Our research in Beirut was a continuation of the fieldwork we had by now completed in London and in Casablanca, investigating how children between the ages of seven and twelve used screen media. In Beirut, rather than going for the conventional sectarian divide, we decided to stratify our field in a way that represented the socio-cultural geography of Beirut. Four key areas of Beirut were chosen, which for us best captured the stratification of the Beirut society: Al-Hamra (a youthful, intellectual/activist cosmopolitan centre, also an attraction for bohemian, subcultural and artistic groups), Dahia (situated in the south of Beirut and a strong foothold of the Lebanese movement Hezbollah), then two suburbs, Aramoun (20 kilometres out of Beirut) and Barja near Saidon (40 kilometres off Beirut). This chapter reflects on our encounters in Dahia, a Hezbollah-governed area, and, to be specific, on the outskirts of a Palestinian refugee camp called Bourj Al Barajneh. Our field work in Dahia consisted of 1 workshop with children living in the area and a family ethnography lasting a total of 3 weeks (Image 3.1).

Our fieldwork in the Dahia is well captured, in hindsight, by Sarah Pink's definition of ethnography as 'reflexive and experiential process through which academic and applied understanding, knowing and knowledge are produced' (Pink 2015: 4–5). Our experience in Dahia with the Refugee children was marked, regardless of our long and

**Image 3.1**  Drawing by a 12-year-old Syrian boy in Beirut representing his future aspirations to 'become a soldier and defend his country Syria'. Permission granted as part of the research material

diligent preparations, by several dislocations: these were methodologi-cal, sensorial, and epistemic. We think it is fair to say that our fieldwork in Dahia had a profound effect on us as scholars and as ethnographers. We had not realised that the incessant mediatisation of suffering had numbed us, at the affective level. It had turned us into disinterested spectators. Nothing had prepared us for the face-to-face *encounter* with the face of the sufferer (or the person doing the suffering), of the suf-ferer's demands to be heard. As such, we felt as though we had been *thrown into* a situation that revealed suffering for us as a kind of onto-logical un-concealment. *Thrownness*, a Heideggerian concept, with which we engage in and thorough which we tell the story of this chapter, had, in our case, morphed from an experiential, sensorial experience to a criti-cal method. Our experience in Dahia is best summarised by Pink's inter-pretation of visual ethnography: 'visual ethnography, as I interpret it, does not claim to produce an objective or truthful account of reality, but should aim to offer versions of ethnographers' experiences of reality that are as loyal as possible to the context, the embodied, the sensory and affective experiences, and the negotiations and intersubjectivities through which the knowledge was produced' (2013: 35).

## THROWNNESS

It is through the double-*thrownness* we encountered as researchers in the field that a wider meaning about structural violence and a complex rela-tionship between method, episteme, and ethics began to emerge. What kind of thrownness are we referring to and in what context? Thrownness is a Heideggerian concept—which finds its origins in the Abrahamic bib-lical tradition: Adam and Eve were thrown into the world after eating from the forbidden fruit of knowledge. In an ontological sense, we are thrown into things—life situations—and this means we must work things out for ourselves—through concern/care—categories that according to Heidegger define our *beingness* in the world. Another form of thrown-ness emerges through the unravelling of our relation to the face of the other—a relation through which we enter an ethical event—an event that reorients our take on ontology—because ontology here is founded on our possible and impossible responsibility towards the other—the other as uniqueness. So, it is through the lenses of these two types of thrown-ness, we will weave the story of our fieldwork in Lebanon and to be pre-cise in the outskirts of the Refugee camp Burj Al Barajneh.

This work is part of a wider three-year research project which explored Arab children's media uses in Beirut, Casablanca, and London. The aim was to move away from discourses of protectionism and victimisation—because of both the Internet's role as game changer in children's media use and related parental control as well as the governmental criminalisation of Arab and migrant children as potential terrorist—and focus on the ways in which children weave their own narratives and take on their media use. In each of the three cities, we conducted ethnography with four families and we spent three weeks with each family. The family viewing ethnography was aided by prompts from the holiday diary we had designed for the children. We would see each family every other day and the diaries were a good way to start conversation. The key questions we were interested in were:

1. How do Arab children in the three cities express narratives about self and the world and what role do digital media play in this process?
2. How do the children articulate ideas of gender, time, and othering?
3. What can we learn about the worldliness of their media and media uses?

We also conducted four workshops in each of the cities. Our samples were organised around difference in class, gender, and geography. In Beirut, as previously explained, we focused on variations in the city's physical and cultural geography, rather than sectarian divisions—even though one quickly learns that sectarianism is part of the fabric and make-up of Lebanese society.

Thrownness into al-Hamra, as a cosmopolitan space, with its avant-garde bars and concept cafés, was seamless. We could have been in parts of London or in a euro-Mediterranean city. Regardless of its uniqueness, its memory of the civil war, its sniper-holed buildings, it still reproduces feelings of sameness—a sameness it shares with other pluralist, open, and energetic spaces of the metropolis.

We develop the argument of this work, which centres around suffering, structural violence, fear, and problems of method, through interplay between the two types of *thrownness*, we have already described: one is inspired by a Heideggerian phenomenological take, which prompts the ethnographer to figure things out for themselves through a process of un-concealment, the other type of thrownness—subscribes to a reading of ontology that is 'accomplished not in the triumph of man over his

condition, but in the very tension in which that condition is assumed'
(Levinas, *entre nous*, 1998: 2). This ontological take is in turn inspired
by a Levinasian ethical human inversion:

> of the in-itself and the for-itself (of "every man for himself") into an ethical
> self, into a priority of the for-the-other—this replacement of the for-itself
> of ontological persistence by an *I* henceforth unique certainly, but unique
> because of its chosenness for a responsibility for the other man…this radi-
> cal turnabout would take place in what I call an encounter with the face of
> the other… he calls to me and orders me from the depth of his defenceless
> nakedness, his misery, his mortality. It is in the personal relationship, from
> me to the other, that the ethical "event", … lead beyond or rise above
> being. (Levinas, *entre nous*, 1998: 202)

## Spatial Thrownness

Bourj-el-Barajneh refugee Camp, situated in Dahia (Southern Suburb
of Beirut), was established in 1948 to accommodate the influx of
Palestinian refugees from what is now Northern Israel. The camp is in
the southern suburb of Beirut and is the most overpopulated camp in
the city. More than 20,000 Palestinian refugees live in the camp; the
camp was initially built to accommodate 10,000 refugees; influx over
several years of different waves of refugees from Iraq, and recently,
Syria into this one square kilometre site has made living conditions in
the camp extremely difficult. The sewage system is regularly flooded
during winter. The camp is run by UNRWA. The security at the entry
of the camp was extremely heavy—it still is: we had to go through
three check points; yet, three months after we finished fieldwork, on
12 November 2015, Bourj-al Barajneh was the scene of two suicide
bombings, killing 37 and injuring 180. Bourj al-Barajneh camp is situated in the town which lent it its name: the town of Bourj Al-Barajneh,
which includes four 'layers' of inhabitants: we think it is important to
explain the complex make-up of Bourj al-Barajneh town, as it situates
us closely to the material everyday realities of the Syrian children we
worked with.

Layer 1: The 'original' inhabitants from *Shi'a* families (and Christian
families until 1984 when they were ethnically cleansed by Hezbollah)
who distinguish themselves from incomers. Historically, they were
pro-feudal leaders who recently gave in to Hezbollah. Layer 2: The
incomers, also *Shi'a* southerners and from the East of Lebanon (*Bekaa*

Valley) who mostly settled irregularly in the late 1970s–1980s due to Israeli occupation and poverty. They are overwhelmingly pro-Hezbollah. The murals of martyrs belong to them. This layer is a mix of poverty, and political clout due to ties with Hezbollah and drug gangs from the *Bekaa* region. Layer 3: The third layer of the town includes the Palestinians inside the camp. This layer of the town lives in extreme poverty, joblessness, crowdedness, and is bullied by Hezbollah and layers 1 and 2. Layer 4: The fourth layer of inhabitants is made of the Syrian refugees who are scattered among areas of groups 1 and 2 and are mostly bullied by them, while they are also subject to frictions with the Palestinians who feel that their plight has been overshadowed by the Syrian crisis.

## EN ROUTE TO FIELDWORK: CHECK POINTS, HAYTISTS, AND THE GAZE OF THE OTHER

Our encounter with Dahia, in all its glory, brought to the fore elements of Arab difference, even strangeness that could only be grasped through the phenomenological encounter. The gaze of the other (haytists: men standing in the corner of little streets), the army by the check point, went right through us—questioning our being there, interrogating us, in minute temporal sequences. Let us be clear about this: We were suspicious outsiders and a possible threat. It is the kind of encounter that no camera lenses can mediate. Distance orientates the affective nature of encounter. The phenomenological encounter of being-there, unlike televisual mediations of phenomena, is a reciprocal process: we were both observing and being observed. It is a reciprocal dynamic of unsettling. But as the gaze moves away from the face of the other into buildings, structures, things, graffiti, another form of unsettlement ensues. Tarik's memories of growing up in Morocco—conjured up the conspicuous display of the king's image in the school, the shops, the university, streets, highways, government offices, the Barber's, the Baker's, and in hotels. In Dahia, imagery and their invasion of space are more diverse, and what you get are images of religious leaders, resistance heroes, martyrs, all men, but diverse, nonetheless. As a stranger and an estranged Arab, what Tarik found eerie was not just the religious and warring nature of the posters or the aura they exhumed, but their size. Gigantic posters of Hezbollah religious leaders and war martyrs are part of a violent strategy; it is an imposition on the eye not to just see but for vision to be filled in its entirety with non-other than images of the religious leader and dead young men of the resistance. The posters denote sacrifice as an idea but also as a proposal for moral and political commitment. The length of the larger-than-life martyr posters serves to immortalise to keep the dead alive in the present, in talk, in folk culture, and in memory.

As we thought of the images of the martyrs and their conspicuous presence/absence, we could not help but take a glimpse into the future of an even more sinister dystopic image of Bourj Al-Barajnah: Hezbollah will have digitalised all the martyr posters so that they can interact, as media of the future, with passers-by: speaking martyrs will remind them of the political cause—how they were killed and how the fight must go on.

On the way to an ethnographic session one day, we looked up from the car window and our eyes caught an 8-metre-long and three-metre-wide poster of a young martyr, dressed in Hezbollah attire. The poster was hanging between the first and second floor. A middle-aged woman, dressed in black, moved almost in slow motion, as she hung the washing on the line—her face intoxicated with pain and sorrow—it's the mother of the martyr—Um Shaheed.

## THROWNNESS INTO THE FACE/GAZE OF THE SUFFERER AS-THE-OTHER: THE MAIMOUN FAMILY

We are in the family's sitting room in a second-floor apartment at the outskirts of the Camp. The room is three metres wide in the middle of which lied a Television that did not work. The room had one window, which was wide open every time we visited, but because of the high temperature and the curtain that remained down to prevent the neighbours looking in, there was not much air. The father, Maimoun, a 35-year-old Syrian from Rif Dimashq, who had suffered a major burn injury at work (a gas banister exploded, as he was trying to fix it), sat facing us throughout the fieldwork visits. Maimoun had to leave hospital after three days only, as his family could not afford the treatment. Maimoun chain-smoked as he listened to us and every time he took a cigarette out, he courteously offered us one. We could only say no so many times for fear of offending him. Maimoun would ritually change the bandage in front of us, each time we visited as if to make a point, revealing severe scalding and a mixture of blood and pus. The noisy electric fan, which was interrupted by power cuts, did not bring much relief. It circulated the stench of burned flesh and cheap cigarettes, as we talked and sipped our tea.

The mother, Aliaa, a 30-year-old Syrian from Aleppo, talked inces-santly about the war, expensive rent and the daily abuse her children had been enduring from the neighbours because they are Syrian, a bur-den on the camp, a burden on the war effort. On one occasion, Mahdi, the eldest at 12, was late for the ethnographic session. When he showed up 30 minutes late, his face was bruised. He had been beaten up at the entry of the camp. We were shocked to see the bruises on Mahdi's face, and wondered whether it made any sense at all to start asking the chil-dren about their media uses. It was within this double-thrownness—and here we need to add at an intersection between two kinds of ontologies and the dilemmas they created for us as ethnographers that our discus-sions took place about war, media, weddings, funerals, music, Charlie Chaplin, Hezbollah media, and black magic.

We designed the diaries in Arabic, with key cultural specificities in mind, but nothing prepared us for suffering as an encounter and certainly nothing prepared us for television as a cadaver—the television took centre stage at the Maimoun family's sitting room, but it was a mere ornament—it was a beautifully adorned cadaver. But it was also a live memorial of a time lost, when the Maimoun family could afford and enjoyed watching television in Aleppo. So, television as a medium, can, in this context, be read as both a dead and a live object; it lies at the intersection between multiple temporalities, a mnemonic and more stable past, a tragic present fraught with death and loss and there is the futural possibility for revival: the revival of television as a screen and a technological object and with it, the revival of a hopeful situation, of a resolution, and a better future. In the Maimoun family household, the mother's mobile phone was *the* tech-nology of communication, *the* technology of entertainment, *the* technol-ogy of negotiation and resourcefulness, hope, and anguish.

Mahdi is 12: He is a mechanic and the main breadwinner since his dad had the accident. He has not been to school for three years—he'd forgotten how to read and write. He has a beautiful voice and wants to become a major star.

Fatin is 10—extremely bright—also unschooled for three years—wants to become a doctor. Zakareya is 7: the youngest—he is the only one going to school—and has a Hezbollah youth membership. Noura is 14: She was engaged whilst we were doing the fieldwork and got married to the son of Syrian refugee living in the camp two weeks after we fin-ished the fieldwork. Racheeda is 15 and has some mental disability. She only smiled and never talked much throughout the fieldwork.

## Thrownness, Suffering, and Ethnography as Stammering

Being thrown into the speech, the gesture and the gaze of the sufferer throw us back to a pre-philosophical moment—a moment that resists analysis and theory and asks different things of us as academics, as ethnographers—this is a situation best described by the anthropologist Veena Das who remarked: 'Perhaps, along with describing the methods of fieldwork in which the researcher has complete control over his field, we should also draw attention to the opposite pole: when society seems to take control of the researcher who simply has to lend himself or herself to become the anonymous space on which the hitherto suppressed knowledge of society inscribes itself' (Das 1985: 5).

The fixation thus becomes with the face of the sufferer, their speech, their analysis of the world/their world. The subjectivity of the researcher here reveals itself as a distorted other, a stutterer—a reverse-post-Lacanian mirror reflection, projecting messiness, fuzziness—a state of suspension rather than coherence or linearity. The encounter with the Maimoun family—invited us much later to rethink the whatness of media—moving from a conventional definition—that of broadcasting/digitality/screen/computer to a more ontological and pluralistic interpretation that considers forms of media as extended bodily organs—as uniqueness where bodily organs become extended forms of technicity—the kind of approach with which Andre Leroi Gourhan grapples in *le gest et la parole* and let's not forget Gilbert Simondon's 'trans-individual' (2018) that treat media and technology as extensions of our humanity. The Maimoun family needed to make their fears part of a collective knowledge and to do that, they used speech, the body, the face, and their surroundings. Their deployment of different communicative strategies all amounts to different forms of media. To limit the worldliness of the media to screen-media—or to limit, in our case, Mahdi, Fatin, and Zakareya and Noura's media uses to the mobile phone, and the music videos, reinforces the power of the present absence: the structural mediation of power and ideology through the poster of the martyr—the religious leader—the poem on the wall—mural art—mourning men and women—the funeral—or what amounts to the aesthetics of structural violence.

In the narrow streets, gigantic images of Hezbollah martyrs (and we are talking about towering 6-, 7-, and 10-meter-long posters, sometimes more) converge with electric wiring. The neighbourhood is a live media spectacle of death—where the dead are more alive than the living and where mourning is suspended in a perpetual state of deferral. The spectacle of death and the deferral of mourning is part of an economy of fear, which normalises death and dying as a structure of feeling about the world—a structure which, on the other hand, camouflages the expansionist politics of Hezbollah in Syria, Yemen, Iraq, Saudi Arabia, and other regions of the Arab world. Structures of violence in this case are concealed by the spectacle that creates them. The normalisation of death and with it, patriarchal and religious ideology, giving it aesthetics, becomes the mechanism through which society, as Veena Das put it, hides truth from itself (Das 1985: 5). Images of martyrs, funerals, mural texts, the hanging wires as media are, in this context, and to use Sapiro's words: an absence of presence (Sapiro 1988: xii in Kleinman 2002: 233); what is left out is the political economy of fear, ideology, and structural violence.

## On Ethnography, the Politics of Pity, Emotion, and Commitment

An engagement with the face of the sufferer as media is an invitation to critique and trouble epistemologies that deny the other and deny us a serious if not an ethical engagement with the uniqueness of the face of the other. It is an invitation to put responsibility at the heart of epistemology. But 'uniqueness'—a term frequently used by Levinas in his engagement with the face of the other—requires some unpacking lest we give it a superficial meaning:

> My problem consists in inquiring into how to reconcile what I call the infinite ethical requirement of the face that meets me, dissimulated by its appearance of the other as an individual and as an object. How to enter into this comparison of incomparables without alienating the faces? For beings are not compared as faces, but already as citizens (or in our case as refugees – our emphasis), as individuals, as a multiplicity in a genus and not as "uniqueness". (Levinas 1998: 205)

Levinas's take on 'uniqueness' exposes a discursive process where the experience of the other (their suffering included) is carefully sequestrated by modernity's instrumental institution, the mediatisation of distant suffering being a key element. Levinas's critique can be extended to other institutions such as economy and to teleologies of becoming such as nationalism that tend to instrumentally sequester the uniqueness of the face of the other into big data, numbers, discourses of citizenship, nationalism, and even pluralism. The ethnographic method has helped us, as ethnographers, to uncover, because of close proximity, the uniqueness of the face of the refugee as other. Levinas' engagement with the face of the other both as an existential necessity and as an impossibility invites us to think of several questions here. The first and most urgent being: now that we have used a method that allowed us to identify the uniqueness of the face of the sufferer, as opposed to encountering sequestered mediations thereof (the ones Plato refers to as the shadows/mere reflections in his cave allegory), what next? Must we not engage at this point with what Boltanski calls the politics of pity, perhaps the politics of compassion, the relationship between knowledge and action. As Luc Boltanski put it, 'it is only when suffering is considered from the stand point of a politics of pity that the question of commitment appears as a problem...As a politics it aspires to generality...But in its reference to *pity* it cannot wholly free itself from the particular case' (p. 10). Boltanski also observes that for a politics of pity to count as politics, it has to avoid the pitfalls of singular suffering—it must be able to convey a plurality of 'situations of misfortune'. Here, for Boltanski, a hyper-singularising through an accumulation of the details of suffering is necessary (p. 12). But does singularity take politics of pity out of the encounter between the ethnographer and the research subject? In our study, it was exactly because of our refusal to hyper-singularise suffering that we encountered the uniqueness of the face of the sufferer. The question, we may also ponder, is: how can such a uniqueness be hyper-singularised? Politics of pity cannot be developed, argues Boltanski, without the 'division and separation between the unfortunates and the fortunate' (p. 13). The separation was, in our case as ethnographers, unescapable even if our encounter with the face of the sufferer was direct. The separation in this case was not determined by spatial distance, but by the researcher and researched divide. Our research and its aims had totally been obliterated by the reality of the unfortunate, a reality that was clearly more urgent than knowledge production. We have, of course, engaged with the family's viewing habits, etc., but this was secondary to letting the sufferer speak. The division in our case was one between two types of commitments: commitment to the field and our role as ethnographers, and the proposal *to* commitment made most powerfully by the sufferer's face and voice. The intention was to observe media uses by Syrian refugee children, but our ethnographic encounter altered our course and so our intended observations of media uses had largely been substituted by observations of suffering. We have by default fulfilled Esther Benbassa's aphorism. In her book, *Suffering as Identity: The Jewish Paradigm*, Benbassa remarks: "In order to learn about the other's suffering, one must observe it' (Benbassa 2010: 24). But in refocusing our attention on suffering and the face of the unfortunate, without any real or practical plans to relieve the sufferer of their suffering, are we not, by default, to misquote Madame Riccoboni (1769 letter to Garrick from Paris), 'readily creating unfortunates to taste the sweetness of feeling sorry for them'? (quoted in Boltanski 1999: 101).

## CONCLUSION

Thrownness is an entangled existential condition that is at once traversal and processual—it is through it that we are able to encounter our humanity—it is affect itself. Thrownness is the process through which we humans encounter the world, joy, suffering, things, feelings, and understanding. It is the process through which we figure things out for ourselves. But it is always in our encountering of the other, the other's face, the other's culture, that thrownness comes to the fore as an existential condition. In reflecting on our encounters in Dahia, we resisted the meaning-making structures that privilege 'objective' truth over thrownness. We championed thrownness as a process and let the affective experience of encountering guide our ethnographic journey. It was Maimoun, Aliaa, and their children that mattered, their faces, voices, and their suffering and not what we could objectively get out of the encounter or the meaning-making process. Our thrownness was traversal and processual. It started out as a condition which then morphed into a critical and affective method. Thrownness has a dual composition: it is at once a condition and a thinking/figuring out process, but each resides in a different temporality. The condition, *being-thrown-in*, is temporally finite, but the figuring-things-out process it prompts is temporally traversal. It has no end point. The figuring out process lingers in time and beyond the eventfulness that created it. Thrownness is the product of an ethical event, where the objective world collides with affective regimes. The figuring out process will persist in lingering as we, as humans and ethnographers, yearn to make sense of who 'we' are.

# BIBLIOGRAPHY

Benbassa, E. (2010). *Suffering as Identity: The Jewish Paradigm*. London: Verso.
Boltanski, L. (1999). *Distant Suffering: Morality Media and Politics*. Cambridge: Cambridge University Press.
Das, V. (1985, June). Anthropological Knowledge and Collective Violence: The Riots in Delhi, November 1984. *Anthropology Today, 1*(3), 4–6.
Das, V. (Ed.). (1990a). *Mirrors of Violence*. Oxford: Oxford University Press.
Das, V. (Ed.). (1990b). Our Work to Cry: Your Work to Listen. In V. Das (Ed.), *Mirrors of Violence* (pp: 345–399). Oxford: Oxford University Press.
Das, V., Kleinman, A., Ramphele, M., & Reynolds, P. (2002). *Violence and Subjectivity*. Berkeley and Los Angeles: University of California Press.
Kleinman, A. (2002). The Violences of Everyday Life: The Multiple Forms and Dynamics of Social Violence. In V. Das, A. Kleinman, M. Ramphele, & P. Reynolds (Eds.), *Violence and Subjectivity*. Berkeley and Los Angeles: University of California Press.
Leroi-Gourhan, A. (1964). *Le geste et la parole*. Paris: éditions albin michel.
Levinas, E. (1998). *Entre Nous, Thinking-of-the-Other*. New York: Columbia University Press.
Pink, S. (2013). *Doing Visual Ethnography* (2nd ed.). London: Sage.
Pink, S. (2015). *Doing Sensory Ethnography* (2nd ed.). London: Sage.
Simondon, G. (2018). *On the Mode of Existence of Technical Objects* (C. Malsapina & J. Rogove, Trans.). London: Univocal.

CHAPTER 4

# Networked World-Making: Children's Encounters with Media Objects

**Abstract** How do screen media transpire through the spatialities, temporalities, and socialities of Arabic-speaking children and their processes of world making? This chapter addresses the complex dynamics of children's media use and preferences by going back to these everyday mediated encounters to unravel the multiple layering of space and time in relation to the enactment of being as an 'Arab' child in the early twenty-first century. The chapter proposes an understanding of media within Latour's (2005) notion of 'objects' as active bearers and explicators of the 'crushing exercise of power'. It also reconciles Latour's Actor-Network Theory (ANT) with a phenomenological understanding of cultural encounters used in this volume. Taking a comparative approach across the three field-sites, the chapter interrogates dominant epistemologies around the TV as a central object/medium/device found in established research on Arabic-speaking children's media use. It opens up the analysis of media use by shifting focus from 'availability' to 'presence', which allows the exploration of the affective connection between the child user and the media-object within the complex temporalities and spatialities involved in their media use. This approach fleshes out the

Excerpts of this chapter were published in Mansour, N. (2018). Unmaking the Arab/Muslim Child: Lived Experiences of Media Use in Two Migratory Settings. *Middle East Journal for Culture and Communication, 11*(1): 91–110. Used with permission from Brill Publishers.

65

social-medial 'assemblages' shaping the agency of Arabic-speaking children and their media uses.

**Keywords** Objects · Network · Spaces · Materialities · Child audiences · Users

## INTRODUCTION

Of those unexpected moments in this field research was an afternoon during the London fieldwork in the summer of 2013. We sat with Sophia and Michael, respectively 12 and 9 years old, to review their entries in the viewing diaries. Reviewing Michael's diary, two entries stood out. The first entry asked respondents to introduce themselves in open-ended prompts. Michael proudly introduced himself as 'addicted to games' (Ethnography 1, London, July 2013).

Michael played games—and one in particular, *Binweevils*—on a tablet he shared with his sister as well as on his parents' smart phones when they allowed him to. He had his own user account for his favourite game and competed with other players across the net. The daily records on the diary showed that he used this game the most, daily, sometimes several times a day, in between other activities he engaged with during his summer days, with much disregard to the large TV set in the living room (Image 4.1).

Another task asked respondents to list the media they used the previous day according to their primary formats of video, audio, and written text.

> *Nisrine*: Michael, what about the audio? You have listed films under audio…
> *Sophia*: Exactly, I told him!
> *Nisrine*: So, what do you mean with it? We usually watch movies. So, it maybe needs to go under video
> *Michael*: No, I mostly listen to movies. When I am in bed, I turn my head round and I listen to them
> *Nisrine*: and who would be watching them?
> *Michael*: Sophia
> *Sophia*: No, I sleep in the other room.
> *Michael*: ok, usually it is Mom and Dad
>
> (Ethnography 1, London, July 2013)

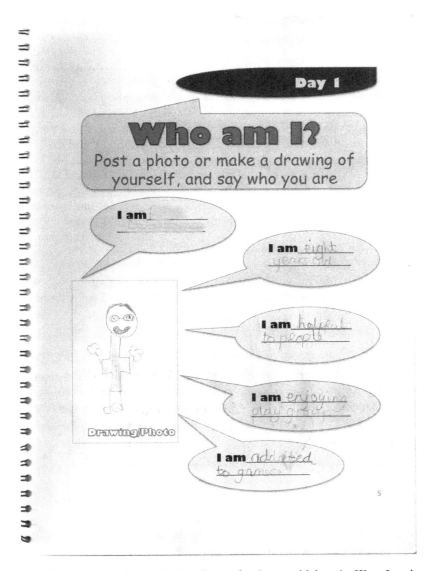

**Image 4.1**  Excerpt from viewing diary of a 9-year-old boy in West London introducing himself as 'addicted to games'. Permission granted as part of the research material

Michael's insistence on 'listening to a film' during his sleep time opened up our imagination to rethink the worlds that children make and occupy through their contemporary media use. Born and raised in London, Michael belonged to a low-income household, where living arrangements were compact. Their home consisted of a small one-bedroom flat that he shares with his parents, sister, and grandmother who divided her time between London and her native village in North Lebanon. The bedroom included a double bed reserved for his parents and a bunker bed for him and his sister. However, it was too crammed for them all, and Michael usually slept on the sofa in the living room, which he shared with his grandmother when she was around. Michael's home was the epicentre of three worlds. First, the virtual world of gaming, accessed through the communal devices available at home, is one that is of most importance to him. Second, the world of unintentional TV viewing, was dictated not much by personal choice, but by the living arrangements and economic condition of his parents. This world defied the rules of socialisation imposed by broadcasting media (Morley 2000). Third, the mnemonic world of his heritage country that he never visited was mediated by the seasonal stay of his grandmother. As such, Michael's home was of phantasmagorical nature where materiality intersected with immateriality to bring everyday notions of existence and being (Morley 2000; Sabry 2010).

Michael's media use shared commonalities with most other child respondents living in the two other field-sites of Morocco and Lebanon. In all three sites, child respondents' homes showed the availability of a range of devices beyond the iconicity of the TV. With this increased availability, children had more access to different media and devices than the literature suggested. They were no different from their peers in other parts of the world, finding various points of access and hopping across them to use their favourite media. As Michael's account revealed, children's use of the media was not only an intentional act of use. Rather, it was enacted through everyday encounters between actors, objects, material, and immaterial spaces, and multiple times. These everyday encounters offer a unique opportunity to decentralise children's media use from a dual monolith, that of media-centric and child-centred approaches.

The emerging multiplicity of children's everyday worlds led us to forego the initial project's focus on the TV as the primary object of study in the literature on Arab children's media use. We also departed from focusing on the media as a primary analytical unit. Through the ethnography, children eagerly shared their favourites with us to watch and play. The viewing diaries and conversations unravelled the intricate connection between media use and the broader social environment. Children were happy to speak about the media; yet, they constantly located them within their broader activities. They spent time telling us about—and noting down—their favourite outings, activities, longings, dreams, and fears. Media emerged as the thread that tied their worlds together. It was no longer possible to analyse children's media use within the confines of the binary of 'media-centric' or 'child-centred' approaches. Their media use was enmeshed within spatialities, temporalities, and socialities that acknowledged, yet exceeded classical notions of intentionality of media use. As Michael's example reveals, preference for a particular medium (games) and actual media use (overheard films) depended as much on the availability of the devices/media as on its 'presence' across the child's temporalities and spatialities within and beyond the household. As Keightley and Pickering (2012: 72) remind us, the 'mnemonic imagination generates movement between the horizons of experience, expectation and possibility. It brings the temporal tenses together and synthesises them productively in order to achieve new meaning in the present'. It is only when these factors were considered that we could understand the processes of action that connected children with the media, inasmuch as how children use the media, as to the social and medial networks through which various media made it through to the children.

This chapter addresses the complex dynamics of children's media use and preferences building on Latour's (2005: 72) insistence that 'objects are […] highlighted not only as being full-blown actors, but also as what explains the contrasted landscape we started with, the overarching powers of society, the huge asymmetries, the crushing exercise of power'. The chapter goes back to these everyday mediated encounters to unravel the multiple layering of space and time in relation to the enactment of being as an 'Arab' child in the early twenty-first century. The chapter reconciles Latour's Actor-Network Theory (ANT) with a phenomenological understanding of cultural encounters used in this volume. At first glance, ANT and phenomenological approaches to cultural studies seem to hold more disparities than parallels. For a start, Latour's sociological grounding is suspicious towards a cultural lens, where 'a culture is simultaneously that which makes people act, a complete abstraction created by the ethnographer's gaze, and what is generated on the spot by the constant inventiveness of members' interactions" (Latour 2005: 168). However, Latour's attack on ethnographers of culture is understood differently when taken within his broader critique of the positivist approaches underpinning the epistemological monopoly applied by 'experts' and which seeks to negate the lived experiences of the researched in favour of constructing facile and packed readings of uncomfortable social phenomena that destabilise the experts' academic dogmas of people-centred versus structure-centred analyses. By stressing the importance of hyphenating actors and networks, Latour is proposing to move away from epistemological hierarchies and account instead for the plurality and complexity of phenomena not least those enacted within everyday encounters. In our case, children's everyday encounters with the media could not present a better chance to explore further these complexities. It is more relevant as Latour early on dispelled the hierarchy between the macro and the micro, the global as a stand-alone pervasive force, and the local, individual action which is often reduced to an ossified 'context' within which respondents are situated. Latour suggests instead to eliminate hierarchies and map actions in terms of 'local' and 'connected' sites of equal physical and symbolic importance (2005: 172). Understood in this way, Latour's notion of connections aligns with an open understanding of cultural encounters as noted by Sabry where the act of encountering coexists in a three-dimensional temporality: (a) the [actual] time of the encounter [...], (b) the cultural time of the encountered [...], and (c) the cultural time of those who do the encountering (Sabry 2010: 10–11). Another seeming area of disparity between phenomenological and ANT is the ontological understanding of being. Heidegger defined Dasein as a state of being or existence, an 'entity which in its Being has this very Being as an issue...' (Heidegger 1927 [1962]: 68). What is at stake here is not only the condition of being, but the very consciousness of being and what it entails in terms of experiencing the world and understanding it. For Latour, being is inherently action-related where 'all the actors do something and don't just sit there' (2005: 128). At the surface, the difference between the two perspectives seems to be about 'being' and 'doing'. However, both philosophies hold two crucial similarities that justify their compatibility. First, for both Heidegger and Latour, being is not reserved only for human actors. Dasein holds a deeper meaning of being-in-the-world, that is being involved in the world and caring for it, which resonates with Latour's understanding of actors as 'free to deploy the full incommensurability of their own worldmaking activities' and our responsibility as researchers to 'cast off agency, structure, psyche, time, and space along with every other philosophical and anthropological category, no matter how deeply rooted in common sense they may appear to be' (2005: 24–25). Both philosophies also rule out the positivist separation between human and non-human beings in relating to world-making. For Heidegger, 'Being is always the Being of an entity', and 'being-in-the-world' brings consciousness that is always about 'something', in the sense that both subjects and objects are animated by consciousness that endows their being (Heidegger 1962: 29). Latour also relies on the term 'entities' to explain societies as 'the bundles of composite entities that endure in time and space', where 'subjectivity is not a property of human souls but of the gathering itself' (2005: 218). In this sense, both phenomenology and ANT are concerned with observing the relevance of various elements that make the encounter. They open up the scope of understanding actors' experiences in relation to objects in space and time, and their overlooked potential of acting as connectors, or mediators within a network, through sites or nodes that reveal the controversies or paradoxes of being and acting in the world.

This chapter builds on these theoretical intersections to tie in the notion of cultural encounter with children's being and doing as intertwined processes of world-making. It considers cultural encounters as phantasmagoric processes of being and doing that contrast different temporalities and spatialities. In the case of our research, the home emerges as the prime site for these processes. Here, David Morley's concern with the home helps to elucidate the importance of the home as a physical and symbolic site for world-making. Morley, quoting Hobsbawm, makes a distinction between 'Home, in the literal sense Heim, chez moi, [which] is essentially private ... [and] belongs to me and mine and nobody else', and 'Home in the wider sense, Heimat [which] is essentially public, Heimat is by definition collective. It cannot belong to us as individuals' (Hobsbawm 1991: 67–68, quoted in Morley 2000). While Hobsbawm's differentiation is useful to articulate notions of home and national identity, it precedes the changing definitions of *Home* induced by the condition of late modernity and characterised by hyper-mediatisation and compression of time and space. Morley asserts that 'the contemporary world is a world of movement and that mobility (both physical and imaginative) is central to our conceptualisation of modernity and its various "posts"' (2000: 9). Morley makes the point of reconceptualising home in light of this contemporariness, quoting anthropologist Mary Douglas's view that home is located but not fixed, and human geographer Doreen Massey's negation of locality as 'few people's... daily lives can be described as simply local. Even the most "local" ... people... have their lives touched by wider events, are linked into a broader geographical field' (Massey, in Morley 2000: 10). Morley's lucid articulation of the contemporary world becomes more pertinent when analysed in light of the accelerated technological advances shaping the very processes involved in the temporalities and spatialities of world-making. Here, Latour's ANT approach is particularly useful in connecting actors and objects—specifically media objects for our interest—through a network of connections, rather than physical localities. The usefulness of the network perspective is to flatten the hierarchies between the global and the local and map them instead as part of the analytical process of revealing the invisibility of the phantasmagoric realm of the home and associated spaces.

Taking a comparative approach across the three field-sites, the chapter interrogates dominant epistemologies around the TV as a central object/medium/device found in established research on Arabic-speaking children's media use. It opens up the analysis of media use by shifting focus from 'availability' to 'presence', which allows the exploration of the affective connection between the child user and the media-object within the complex temporalities and spatialities involved in their media use. This approach allows to flesh out the social-medial 'assemblages' shaping the agency of Arabic-speaking children's media use.

But how does the media transpire through the spatialities, temporalities, and socialities of Arabic-speaking children and their processes of world-making? This chapter aims to explore children's media use through a network analysis approach that accounts for both actors and objects as elaborated by Latour (2005).

The first section of the chapter delves into children's temporalities and the dynamic and intricate link between media use and cultural time. The second section maps out the multiple spatial layering of media use across the social spaces inhabited by the children. The third section excavates children's media objects at home, tracing significant changes in the affective relationship between children and the media available to them. The chapter wraps up with concluding remarks.

## TEMPORALITIES, SPATIALITIES, AND THE ELUSIVENESS OF AVERAGE MEDIA USE

As we moved across the three sites, we initially designed the research to account for a seasonal dichotomy between winter/school time and summer/vacation time. Stretching over three consecutive summers between 2013 and 2015, the fieldwork intended to reflect children's availability out of the school calendar with the aim to optimise the capture of their unrestricted use of the media.

For children, summer equated freedom from school. The school calendar months were the heaviest period of the year for both children and parents. Children's time and energy (as well as their parents') were effectively taken up by the school during the day and homework in the evenings. In most cases, parents were diligent in monitoring their children's homework, leaving them with hardly any time to use the media. They restricted their leisure time, including media time, to a minimum, usually amounting to one or two hours of media use per day. Yet, the assumptions around the summer/winter divide in media use were challenged when we looked in detail into children's summer schedules.

### *Diasporic Connections*

Summer time was an opportunity for children to step out from their London world and connect with their countries of heritage. International travel was mostly destined towards countries of heritage rather than to unrelated tourist destinations. Researched families of North African heritage could only afford such trips every two or three years. They tended to travel by land to Morocco or Algeria, stopping by briefly in Spain for sightseeing on their way there. During these trips, children deeply sensed the collision of their two worlds. Salma, a 12-year-old girl of Algerian heritage, had mixed feelings about her heritage country (Creative Workshop 1, London, July 2013). She described Algeria as 'different, people there don't treat me as one of them. I don't speak Arabic, so it is hard to communicate'. While Salma identified more closely with London, she was frustrated with her state of in-betweenness: 'In Algeria they consider me British, and in London they consider me Algerian'. She resorted to small embodied mnemonic practices to ease her loneliness there: 'whenever I feel homesick while I am there [in Algeria], I blow bubbles in my chewing gum. This is what I do in London, so blowing bubbles there makes me feel that I am home'. At the overlaps between two worlds that did not accept her fully, Salma summoned her mnemonic practices to create a home for herself that she encountered in the action of blowing bubbles in her chewing gum.

These trips exposed children to an array of cultural encounters that intertwined their media and social experiences and formed their world-making. Amina and her sister Dania were two sisters of Moroccan heritage, aged seven and twelve, respectively. They were both immersed in their London world. They spoke only English and listened to Western music, in particular English-Irish pop boy-band *One Direction*. Amina was also a devotee of *Tracy Beaker*, a popular TV show about an orphan child who is finding her way through the foster care system in the UK. For Amina, Tracey Beaker was a symbol of subversion, the underdog who tricked the powers of the British foster care system. Through the sessions, Amina introduced us to the overlaps she experiences between her London and Moroccan worlds:

> *Nisrine*: Do you use Skype?
> *Amina*: yes, I call my auntie, my mom's sister. She lives in Morocco. We always go to her house to sleep over. But I get scared to sleep there. We always go there but we come back to sleep at home
> *Nisrine*: you talk to her much?
> *Amina*: yes, when she calls on the computer. Tititatataaa (skype call tune). This sound hurts my ears
> *Nisrine*: So, whom do you speak to other than your mom's sister?
> *Amina*: Only my mom's brother and her crazy sister. Last time she came on...
> *Dania*: She has a spirit in her
> *Amina*: she hits us sometimes when we get her stuff
> *Dania*: she is possessed
> *Amina*: she hits us when we get her... she tells us she wants chocolate. Then my mom says ok I will bring you some and then she gets angry. They took her away. My auntie has her husband. Her husband beats her and then they fight.
>
> (Ethnography 2, London, July 2013)

In another session, we discussed the content of popular media with Amina, Dania, and their father:

*Tarik*: what about Rihanna? What do you think of her?

*Father*: (To Dania) Do you remember what you told me about her?

*Dania*: yes... (to Tarik) do you know the Illuminati?

*Tarik*: The Illuminati society?

*Dania*: Yes. She is in it.

*Tarik*: And how do you know that?

*Dania*: it was on YouTube. They put it on YouTube. They showed how Michael Jackson died and they showed Beyoncé how she took part in it and how she said she wanted to be part of it

*Nisrine*: I am not familiar with it. Can you explain it to me?

*Dania*: There is like... I don't really know how... Beyoncé she like... they sign like a form and they believe in the ... devil... and they get money for it. They get a lot of money. And if they don't want to be in it, they die. Like Michael Jackson said that there was a guy part of the illuminati, a manager at the music department. So Michael Jackson [exposed him and] said that he was a devil. And then that's how Michael Jackson died apparently. Not the nurse [doctor]. This is how he died.

*Tarik*: so how did you know about it?

*Dania*: It was on Facebook. And they say his family got the money. Also Beyoncé, do you see the song Crazy in Love. You see when they crashed the car, Beyoncé was driving that car, and then the devil came out to her. And she was in the car and she died. So, basically they say there is a new Beyoncé now.

*Tarik*: and all this is on Facebook?

*Dania*: Yeah. And you know. And they do crazy stuff to them. Like Beyoncé she used to wear long dresses.... [but now she wears too revealing clothes]

*Father*: and what about that sign?

*Dania*: yes, there are pictures of Michael Jackson and Beyoncé and Jay Z doing this sign (she locks her fingers in a triangle shape) and it's the devil 666

*Father*: also Rihanna wore that jacket with the black and white sign. And they say it is the sign. She was wearing it in the last interview

*Amina*: Aaaarrrhhhhh [scared moans]

*Nisrine*: Oh! what's happening, are you scared?

*Amina*: yeah

*Dania*: Jay Z, Beyoncé, Rihanna, Michael Jackson, they all do this sign

*Tarik*: I never saw Michael Jackson do this sign

*Dania*: There is a picture of him when he was still black, when he was young and there is a concert of Jay Z where he keeps doing the triangle sign and puts it on his eye, and all the fans started doing it as well. And Miley Cyrus is in it now.

*Nisrine*: So, what does it mean to be in it?

*Dania*: you sell your soul to the devil. And you get lots of money for it. And they have to do what the [Illuminati] ask them to do. It they tell them to … like Michael Jackson you have to turn yourself white, he's got to do it. If they tell you you have to wear revealing outfits, you have to do it. Anything they say. And this is how the shooting at schools happened. And the two buildings [Twin Towers] happened.

*Nisrine*: Who tells them that?

*Dania*: I don't know… It's the managers of the music departments. It happens with every good singer

*Amina*: Oh, I don't want to be a singer anymore

*Nisrine*: So, who are your favourite singers?

*Amina*: Dania, is Jesse J in the Illuminati?

*Dania*: No.

*Amina*: That's my favourite singer then [laughs].

(Ethnography 2, London, July 2013)

The accounts of the Londoner-children speak of the intricate processes of world-making that involve intricate consciousness of the encounters unwrapping their being and doing. Dania and Amina invited us to their phantasmagoric home which was weaved through the threads of three worlds, their London-world, their heritage Moroccan world, and the near-distant US/UK pop celebrity world. These threads formed a connective network texturised at once with a manifest presence of digital technology—Skype, Youtube, and Facebook, inherited notions of mental health, paranormal activities, and domestic gender politics, and fascination with and heavy media use with Western popular culture and capitalist domination and devil worship conspiracy theories.

The digital realm connected their phantasmagoric home to both ends of hidden phenomena that the children unravelled. Their experiences ranged from the very personal, as in the case of their 'possessed' aunt, to the far more distant and mediated threat of devil worship. For them, both states of demons possessing their aunt, and the devil coming out of Beyoncé before being 'replaced' by producers coexisted side by side, were equally powerful and largely unquestioned.

The more 'local' nature of their aunt's 'possession' seemed to be contained within distressing but benign manifestations of individual 'craziness' that affect a distant family member. In contrast, the more 'global' or distant nature of the Illuminati devil worship conspiracy theory came rich with details, evidence, and speculations reflecting the abundance—and authority—of pop media sources on the topic, and the centrality of the digital realm in bringing these connections to presence at the finger-tips of East Londoner children. This presence allowed for the occupation of not only the children's imagination, but also that of the whole fam-ily, extending to their father. As researchers, we initially interpreted the concern with the Illuminati threat as part of the Islamophobia anxiety associated with it. As we were discussing this episode, we asked them if they encountered any religious discrimination at school. The girls and their father rebuffed it and confirmed that it was not an issue for them. Rather, the father's interest in the Illuminati case was more out of a con-cern with the degraded morals of pop music. As an amateur guitar player, he was a big fan of classic rock and especially Bob Dylan. His issue was with the commercialisation of pop culture and the celebrity cult that his daughters were exposed to. For the girls, it was more of a fascina-tion with the celebrity culture, which matters to them most at this age (Projansky 2014). The distant world of celebrity was very close to them as they tried to emulate it. It touched the core of their beings as they explored their creativity and talent at this age. The power of Illuminati threat was powerful in tying glamour and flippant musical tracks with capitalist enslaving resulting from devil worship. It remodelled their musical tastes accordingly and penetrated deep into their aspirations of becoming—in this case, becoming a singer.

## 'Local' Connections

Compared to migrant children, one would assume that non-migrant children such as in Morocco and Lebanon would have a more stable optimal media use in the summer time. Not until we considered the intra-national socialities connecting people to their heritage towns did we encounter the in-country fluidity of networks. In Lebanon, visits to the family's hometown within their own country were quite popular. The compact size of Lebanon made distances and travel costs managea-ble. Families visited their hometowns during the summer breaks as well as during short school breaks. In Morocco, internal travel was more of a financial strain due to the vastness of the country. Most families could afford it only once a year during the summer break.

During these visits, children spent time in an extended home, either at the parents' or relatives' homes. Lina was a 10-year-old girl of mixed Lebanese and Syrian heritage. She was born and grew up in Saida, the sec-ond largest city in Lebanon and was completely immersed in the Lebanese social fabric. Lina regularly visited her Syrian grandparents who lived near the capital and stayed over for a few days in a row. Lina was also a big animal lover with particular fondness to cats. In her parents' big garden, she took care of generations of stray and domesticated cats, feeding them and communicating with them in a special language that she invented. She also had a fertile imagination and knack for storytelling. In her pastime, Lina created an imaginary world of cats that she called Bisbis (Arabic for kitty) Land:

> Goldie is the head of Bisbis land. Pinky is his sister. She married him then she divorced him. Now she has children. Before she also had children; she gives birth all the time. Before Bisbis family, there is Tutu. Coconut Tutu gave birth and aunt Tutu married Coucou Moucou and gave birth to Panda. [...] They live in Bisbis Land where there is war. In Goldie's area, there is no war. I have a house there. [...] there is cat land where they say Meow, Meow only. There is Minay; it's an island with small black things. We took it from the PlayStation. There is a game where you travel and they Minay all the time; so, we called it Minay Island. It has a boat and all of them are black creatures who say Minay. [...]. There is a TV channel on Bisbis Land where they have adverts for cats. there was a revolution and they changed the ruler. He came to Lebanon and sent an army. Part of Lebanon became Bisbis Land. [...] After the death of Jim, the wizard took the throne and ruled badly, He started to change the Lebanese [people] into cats and Bisbis land did not love this so they made a revolution against him. The army had to send them into prison.
>
> (Ethnography 9, Lebanon, August 2015)

As Lina recounted the story of Bisbis Land, she revealed a world that she crafted out of direct experience/fondness with cats, her deep experiences of the media system—playstation, TV, adverts—and her personal exposure to traumatic political events affecting her immediate relatives and mediated through the adults' everyday concerns with and discussions of the Syrian conflict. Lina expressed her talent for story-telling by drawing on the liminality of physical, digital, and affective spaces that create the home. Her consciousness of the Syrian conflict was not much of a 'reflexive' account; rather, it was enacted by the intertextuality of the worlds she navigated in her everyday life. The phantasmagoric world that Lina created through *Bisbis* Land enmeshed fiction with facts to articulate a poetics of contemporary Arab childhood where time, space, and sociality were intrinsically shaped by children's access to and use of the media. These connections spoke of the variability of children's media and social worlds that ethnographically defies the theoretical uniformity of 'average users'.

## EVERYDAY SPACES AND MEDIA USE

### *The School: Classmates and Mnemonic Relatives as London's Main Socialities*

Beyond the seasonal divide, children spent the bulk of their time moving across a variety of habitual social spaces outside the home. The ethnography captured the children's inhabitation of these spaces in relation to the home in order to destabilise its default position as the centre of children's social and media worlds. Children identified strongly with the school as a hub of their social worlds. It stood as a significant site outside the home that children inhabited daily for at least two-thirds of the calendar year. Yet, its potential for sociality and access to various formal and informal aspects of media use varied significantly across the three sites.

In London, children had an overall favourable affinity with school. They enjoyed the subjects of study and found the load of homework manageable. They particularly enjoyed the activity-based pedagogic approach which mainly consisted of school projects requiring online research. For this purpose, schools were equipped with computer labs that children used on a daily basis and complemented any need for further research through available devices at home. Media use was integrated into the daily lives of children through the school–home continuum. The school was also a site for them to negotiate power relations and challenge authority. Teachers enjoyed great popularity among children, with a few exceptions. In a creative workshop (Creative Workshop 2, London, July 2013) with North African Londoner children, one participant complained that teachers tend to wrongfully accuse students of mischief during class to which all participants agreed. When asked about possible solutions, they suggested installing a CCTV camera in class that would monitor, not the children, but the teachers and provide children with proof against the teacher's claims when necessary. The extent to which this solution was applicable does not take away from the fact that children enjoyed a strong sense of agency to challenge authority in comparison to other sites.

Most importantly for the London site, the school was the most significant institutional and communicative space where children formed their opinions and practices in relation to their social worlds and negotiated their Arab/Islamic identity within the UK's multicultural model. At a creative workshop with North African children aged 10–12 years, we had the following discussion on religious practices:

*Tarik*: So why do you wear the headscarf?
*Farida and Salma*: To show respect.
*Amin*: To show you are a proper Muslim.
*Kamal*: To show that you believe in God.
*Ahmed*: So, men won't see your hair.
*Salma*: My mom doesn't wear a headscarf. Only me and my bigger sister.
*Tarik*: So, then your Mom would not be classed as Muslim because she is not wearing a headscarf, as Amin is saying?
*Salma*: She is a Muslim ... I am a better Muslim when I (first person) wear it.
*Tarik to Salma*: So, if your mom is not wearing the headscarf, did your dad ask you to wear it?
*Salma*: Nooo, I asked for it.
*Tarik*: So why did you wear it?
*Farida*: To follow her sister.
*Salma*: No! I wanted to do it and she is only 11 months older.
*Tarik*: Did you father ask you to?
*Salma*: No, I *chose* to wear it. I was influenced by... the public surrounding....
*Farida*: Friends...
*Salma*: yeah friends at school.

(Creative Workshop 1, London, July 2013)

In an ethnographic session, Kifah, a 12-year-old boy of mixed British and Palestinian heritage, confirmed the significance of the school in negotiating his identity. He noted significant differences between his old school and his new one, which he was particularly happy to join:

In my old school [my friend] and me we were the only Muslims in class. In my new school it's like 90% Muslims. [...] it makes a difference because when we fast, they could understand it more. In my old school, I couldn't fast, because they make us eat. They don't make us but they'd rather we eat... But at my new school they let us fast.

(Ethnography 3, London, July 2013)

At school, religious education (RE) was part of the curriculum. However, it did not bring much excitement to Kifah and his friends. Kifah was born of a Muslim Palestinian father and a Catholic British mother. He recounted that he was a Muslim because his parents jointly decided for him to join his father's religion. He knew little about Islam and was keen on learning more about it at school. Instead, his school required children to learn about religions other than their own in order to gain multicultural exposure. Kifah was not impressed with this approach: "They don't get much into it. Say for Chinese New Year, teachers tell us: let's do something about it, like Chinese people do". He summed up what he learned as follows:

> Well, Muslims can't eat pork and can't drink [alcohol] and can't smoke. Well they can smoke cigarettes, but it's better to smoke shisha... because it's more holy or something... Christianity, basically you can't kill or say 'oh my god'. Yes, that's in the 10 commandments, it's Christianity. I don't know a lot about them... Judaism mostly the same as Muslims, but not exactly the same. I don't know that much, but I know it's similar but not the same to Muslims. Buddhists, they are also similar to Muslims, but not the same. They believe in Buddha and they think if they rub his tummy it will bring them wealth.
>
> (Ethnography 3, London, July 2013)

This multicultural pedagogic framing engaged children in simplistic ethnic stereotyping rather than an exploration of belief itself. At school, religious identity was also a significant marker among peers. Kifah recounted how religion is embedded in the process of making friends at his new school. In particular, he mentioned Daniel, one new friend whom he described as funny, and sharing similar interests with like PlayStation, Ping-Pong, and basketball:

> *Nisrine*: do you talk with Daniel about Palestine?
> *Kifah*: Yes, because he is Jewish, and I've said to him that I'm Muslim
> *Nisrine*: is it important for you guys to know each other's religions?
> *Kifah*: Not really, I don't care if anyone is Jewish, but once we make friends, we say which religion we are. After we make friends.
> *Nisrine*: What do you think about him being Jewish?
> *Kifah*: I think that's fine. I don't care about anybody being any religion. We want to know. But no one really cares if you are Jewish or Muslim.
>
> (Ethnography 3, London, July 2013)

### *The* Derb *and the* Cyber: *The Moroccan Neighbourhood as Communal Mediated Space*

In Morocco, the school was a dominant site that brought the least desirable affinity to children. Children also had little faith in the national pedagogic system. They distinguished between public schools which constitute the majority of the schooling system in Morocco, and the more recent private ones. Participants in a creative workshop had mixed views about the pedagogic value of either system. In both types of schools, they complained about the severe disciplining practices used by teachers, which included corporal punishment and bullying from teachers. Omar, an 11-year-old boy explained, "the teacher stacks four wooden rulers on top of each other and laps us with them" (Ethnography 5, Casablanca, July 2014). Private schools, a relatively recent addition to the educational system, was considered a sign of affluence that not many could enjoy. Yet, some children considered them profit-driven and aiming to cash on their students by relaxing their marking standards, as Soraya, a 10-year-old mentioned, 'in private schools, teachers don't care about your work, the parents bribe them to give their children higher grades' (Creative Workshop 4, Casablanca, July 2014). In both systems, Media facilities were dated with no computer access or use. While a few schools had libraries stacked with books, the administration often banned access for children in order to preserve books from wear and tear.

With the school as restrictive space, Moroccan children favoured and made use of many more alternative spaces than any other children in the two other sites. The neighbourhood or 'Derb' was a significant site of sociality owing to particular local housing arrangements and solidary social relations. In Morocco, the Derb featured as a dominant site for children's everyday summer time across the socio-economic spectrum. Respondents of both genders enjoyed playing there for hours with their neighbouring peers without direct parental supervision. It was the place where children played hide and seek, skipped rope, kicked the football, and also chatted about their favourite shows, computer games, and football teams. In some parts of congested and low-income areas of the Old Medina, the Derb contained some risks for children. Omar and Marwan's mother always kept an eye on her two 10- and 12-years-old sons while they played there: "The Derb is marred with young druggies. They are bad influence. Some of them bully their mothers and families and it is something I don't want my children to pick up on" (Ethnography 5, Casablanca, July 2014). In order to optimise her children's learning chances, the mother pooled her meagre resources and signed up her older son Marwan at the nearby public library. Marwan loved the library and went there regularly to use the internet facilities and borrow books for him and his brother Omar to read at home.

The *Derb* contained other risks that could have direct impact on children's sociability. Hanin, an 11-year-old girl, lived in a small one-bed flat in another part the Old Medina with her parents and older brothers (Ethnography 6, Casablanca, July 2014). Hanin was studious, with the dream to become a dentist when she grows up. Her father was a carpenter and had his workshop at the roof of the building and thus spent much time with his daughter during the summer days. Hanin stayed at home most of the time. She enjoyed watching an array of shows and films on various Arab satellite channels, in addition to Zee Aflam, an Indian Dubai-based channel featuring Bollywood films. When asked if she played in the *Derb*, Hanin said that she prefers to stay indoors. Her father later took us to the side and explained that the alley where they live was not safe for her (Image 4.2):

> Opposite to our front door, there is a buzzing spiritual 'clinic' with a practicing a traditional *Sheikh* (healer). The clinic is constantly crowded by people coming to seek remedies for their or their loved ones' mental ailments. This poses a problem for us. You see Hanin has got a special feature in her physical make up that puts her at risk... The lines on Hanin's palms are traced in an unusual way, which in some beliefs is a sign that she is a 'special' child who brings spiritual healing. Such a rare trait is highly sought after by traditional healing practitioners and patients who would go to lengths to exploit it. We worry that if Hanin mingles in the *Derb*, she will be spotted... She could be abducted and used in healing practices. So, we always ask her to stay indoors and we accompany her when going out to our friends and relatives.
>
> (Ethnography 6, Casablanca, July 2014)

Despite these restrictions, Hanin enjoys some supervised quality time outdoors. On one occasion, she and her father took us up to the roof to show us the workshop and the beautiful sea view. On one of the laundry railings was a wetsuit drying in the sun and a small surfboard next to it on the floor. The father explained that Hanin was a keen swimmer and surfer. He regularly took her to the sea to enjoy a swim. Hanin wore the scarf and the wetsuit was perfect for her to enjoy her hobby.

The *Derb* included another significant site—especially for boys. The '*Cyber*', or the old style internet café, still widespread in Morocco as in many other countries. These *Cyber* spaces allowed mixed gender and some girls mentioned visiting it occasionally. The *Cyber* was mostly populated by boys and men who go there and surf the net without much

**Image 4.2** Image of the front door of spiritual practice in Casablanca's Old Medina facing the home of one respondent. Permission granted as part of the research material

censorship. Yet, children—and parents—did not seem to raise questions as to the safety of children as in the account of Marwan and Omar:

> *Marwan*: yes, there is a cybercafé where boys play too.
> *Nisrine*: What do you do there?
> *Marwan*: Ohhh you can do *everything*. We go with friends and play a football game, so we are like three or four sitting on different computers competing against each other. We also watch movies there. I saw *Mission Impossible* the other day.
> *Omar*: I love going on Facebook there.
> *Nisrine*: So, you have a Facebook account?
> *Omar*: Yes! I have 900 friends. All over the world. We speak [i.e. type chat] in Moroccan using French letters.
> *Nisrine*: So, they understand Moroccan?
> *Omar*: Yes, they are all Moroccan living abroad.
> *Marwan*: I love that we get to know so much about the world through them.
> *Tarik*: At what age are you allowed to go there to play?
> *Marwan*: All ages are allowed, what you have to do is to pay money and nothing else is essential than this.
> (Ethnography 5, Casablanca, July 2014)

At two dirhams per hour (0.20 USD), the *Cyber* was an affordable leisure activity for children of all ages. Omar and Marwan loved going to a nearby *Cyber* and typically spent one to two hours every day depending on their available pocket money. They mainly played football games with friends, surfed the internet, and used social media like Facebook.

### *Networked Familial Socialities: Relatives as an Extended Connected Home*

For Lebanon-based children, the school symbolised a dominant site for intensive education. Children and parents complained from the 'tons of homework' and that all they did during the winter was "study, study, study". Parents confirmed that they wanted to provide their children with the best education, so they enrol them in a 'good school because the rest is of terrible quality'.[1] The predominantly private schooling system in Lebanon brings deep social inequalities that marginalise disadvantaged student groups such as refugees (Chatty et al. 2014). Parents who can afford private schooling closely supervise their children with long sessions of homework and relentless pressure to get good grades during the academic year.

With such competitive environment, children did not particularly have close connections with their schoolmates. Most named one close friend at school; yet, they counted several ones that they 'hated' because they were constantly 'mean' to them. At several instances during the ethnography, playground politics were discussed at length as children recounted their grievances towards some of their classmates who excluded them from group play, ignored them, connived with other classmates, and bragged about their possessions and looks. These grievances were particularly distressing for children and often parents were involved in mitigating them.

Of the three research sites, Lebanese parents came across as the most involved in their children's lives, dictating the smallest aspects of their education, activities, and relations with their peers. Parents also organised children's socialities closely with extended family. One example is Yasmin's family who lived in one of the suburbs of Beirut (Ethnography 10, Beirut, August 2015). The suburb was nestled in the middle of pine trees and greenery, setting it aside from main public transport routes. Despite the inviting scenery, the family did not have any interaction with their neighbours. Parents mentioned that the neighbourhood was not safe and was filled with 'strangers' who could not be trusted—referring to young Syrian refugee men who lived there due to its affordability.

During our visits in the hot summer days, Yasmin and her younger brother stayed indoors, playing games on the tablet or doing their summer homework. On their parents' instructions, they did not venture outdoors and did not even make use of the large balcony to play. Both parents were dedicated to their children's well-being. They pooled all their resources to fund their children's education at a 'very good school that holds high standards of education'. Their financial situation was tight, and they had to forego satellite and internet subscription at home to reduce running costs. The wife, a homemaker who attended to all aspects of the children's schooling and upbringing, did not drive nor own a car, so their movement depended on her husband's availability.

Yasmin's father worked two full-time jobs with hardly any weekend breaks to afford the school fees for his children in central Beirut. He managed to steal some little free time daily to spend with his children by devising the routine to drive them at lunch time to his wife's extended family home in the city. This routine applied during both summer and winter times. Every afternoon, the father drove his wife and children to her parents' place to spend the rest of the day until he picks them up on his way back at around midnight. The grandparents' home was connected both to satellite TV and the internet. Children did their homework at their grandparents' place and spent the rest of the time with their cousins surfing the net and watching TV there. This way, Yasmin's home extended to that of her grandparents'. She loved going there and hanging out with her cousins for hours on end. This social organisation was also noted with more affluent families, although at the rate of a few days a week rather than daily. Parents tended to organise leisure activities for their children and cousins such as trips to the beach, water parks, cycling clubs, or the cinema. These activities were all commercially driven and costly; yet, many families used them as there are very few free public leisure spaces to use in Beirut.

## Affective Materialities, Availability, and Presence

### The Home as Site for 'Arab' Media Transition

For all families across the three sites, the home was the common denominator, the main hub of activity where children's worlds unfolded and channelled in a communicative loop across the various other spaces and with various actors. The technological set-up in researched households spoke of the generational transition into the digital era. Households and living arrangements within and across the three sites offered a wide diversity of media devices and use.

London-based families had an average of two children in the household. Depending on their economic situation, they lived in one-, two- or three-bedroom flats or houses. Homes were tuned to multiple devices including the TV, laptops, tablets, consoles, and phones. The gap in children's access to the media was relatively low. For instance, Kifah, living in an affluent three-bedroom house, counted four TV sets in his home in addition to a laptop, a games console, a high-end tablet, and a personal smartphone. At the lower end of the financial ladder, Sophia and Michael counted a TV set, a low-end tablet, and their parents' smart phones. The family laptop broke down and could not be replaced due to financial strain. However, the children relied on the school's facilities to use computers during school time. With the exception of Sophia and Michael, children either had their own bedrooms or shared them with one sibling.

In Casablanca, home space and media devices were scarcer than in the two other sites. Accommodation among the poorest families, such as Omar and Marwan, consisted of a windowless 3×3 meters all-purpose room with shared toilet facilities across the building. In the minute space, the family had one small old TV set in addition to the parents' basic low-cost smart phones. At the other end of the spectrum, upper-middle class children resided in two-bedroom flats with a TV set, and their own high-end tablet and smartphone. Children in lower-middle income households had one TV set, access to their parents' low-cost smart phones, and occasionally, a desktop reserved to the older male siblings with little access by the younger siblings. On average, households consisted of a one-bedroom flat, indicating distinctly more communal living arrangements in Morocco than the other two sites. With most families, female members of the households (mothers and daughters) slept in the bedroom, while males slept in the living room.

Lebanon-based households had similar living arrangements to those in London. Children had their own rooms or shared them with siblings, with another bedroom room reserved for their parents. Children had access to a broad range of devices, consisting of TV sets, parents' phones, tablets, laptops. Children in Lebanon had additional access to DVDs, which parents stocked for their children in addition to or in replacement of TV time. Parents found that 'there isn't much on TV these days, we prefer to select good material for them to watch'. Most of the DVD content consisted of Disney fairy tale classics in addition to more recent hits such as *Frozen*.

### The TV Dethroned: Availability and Purposeful Media Use

The availability of a broad range of devices within the home reflected the current technological media transition, with different implications for parents and children. Parents were attuned to the TV and used it as their default medium, with varying opinions as to the usefulness of its content. In London, parents tended to consider the TV as an important medium connecting their children to their heritage countries. As Sophia and Michael's mother mentioned:

> Yes [TV] is great! We get Lebanese and Arab satellite [channels] here so children can practice their Arabic a bit. Otherwise they wouldn't speak it at all. You should see them, they love some Lebanese comedy and variety shows, and they watch them with us, especially when their grandma is here [for half the year] she has it on all the time. Between us, this is also all we watch, we never switch to British TV.
>
> (Ethnography 1, London, July 2013)

Parents in London were more familiar with Arab than British television networks and had satellite subscription to several pan-Arab networks such as Al Jazeera, in addition to national channels such as MTV Lebanon, and 2M, the Moroccan satellite channel. Sophia and Michael effectively echoed their mother's claim and enthusiastically hummed the opening credits for *Mafi Metlo*, one long-standing Lebanese satire show. They also named several Lebanese pop singers and actors. However, the TV did not bring closer understanding to their country of heritage as their parents hoped.

> *Sophia*: I never watch the news. I do watch it once my father is watching, about Syria and stuff but I don't really watch it. I forget much of it. There is a lot of war in Syria. I can't understand why. Children are getting killed. What where they doing?! It's sad for people to die. Syrian people are nice. It's like WW2 but not WW2 and definitely not WW1 or WW0
> *Nisrine*: do you know where Syria is?
> *Sophia*: No.
> *Nisrine*: do you know where Lebanon is?
> *Sophia*: I forgot.
> *Nisrine*: Syria is next door to Lebanon.
> *Sophia*: So, there is war in Lebanon...
> NISRINE: Not really. Lots of Syrian refugees fled to Lebanon
> *Sophia*: So [her paternal hometown] has war?
> NISRINE: No.
> (Ethnography 1, London, July 2013)

Despite being heavily exposed to the TV through her Lebanese parents and grandma, Sophia's geo-political knowledge about her home country was sketchy, to say the least. Although the TV brought some affinity with her heritage country's popular culture, she was more concerned with conflict as a universal distressing condition affecting children, which was a recurring theme across most children in the three sites. Furthermore, although the TV was available as a main source of Lebanese content, Sophia's and Michael's interest in it was minimal compared to their strong engagement with British and Western content that they gained through their school and friends' networks as well as various online platforms they used.

The availability of the TV was not a synonym for its importance among children, as the example of Nada reveals. Nada was a 10-year-old girl from North African heritage, born and raised in London. In one of the creative workshops held in a North London Mosque, Nada surprised us and other participants by mentioning that she did not have a TV:

> *Tarik*: How many TVs do you have at home?
> *Nada*: I haven't got a TV.
> *Tarik*: At all?
> *Nada*: No. not at all.
> *Tarik*: why?
> *Nada*: Because sometimes stuff pop up… well my mom says some things pop up. Music or something, things pop up in the middle. You know every advert has got music in the middle. So, we are not allowed to watch it. But I have got a laptop and a computer, so I watch on my own.
> (Creative Workshop 1, London, July 2013)

For Nada's parents, music and 'things that pop up' were considered 'haram', or undesirable practices, among observers of strict Islamic teachings. It was a surprising and exceptional practice that we have not encountered with any other children elsewhere across the three sites. Nada's account encapsulated the gap between parents and children at the level of both morality and technology. She easily subverted her parents' moralities and technological limitations, by seeking resort in her laptop that her parents bought her. Nada's parents did not apply parental control on her computer. This might be due to the fact that they were not well-versed with digital technology or they assume that she was only using her laptop for homework. She was familiar with some shows like *Family Guy*, a cartoon series about a dysfunctional American family and classified as inappropriate for children under 12 years of age due to its controversial content. Nada was no different from the other children in the creative workshop who at once were observant Muslims and fans of Family Guy's direct satire of religious and social conformity.

In Morocco, the TV had more prominence than the other two sites. With the scarcity of other devices and platforms, it was valued as a communal entertainment activity that children enjoyed with their parents. Parents intently watched TV and had it switched on in the background all day long. For instance, during our visits to Omar and Marwan, the TV was constantly switched to Al-Jazeera channel. *Ghaza Toqawim* (Gaza Resists) was a special feature that the network ran all day long during the last Israeli attack on Gaza in 2014. It featured live news coverage of the offensive with graphic images of bombings, devastation, and killings of children. These images were widespread and affected all researched children in Morocco. In one creative workshop, children expressed their sorrow for Gazan children who are killed en masse:

*Nisrine*: do you watch the news?
*Boy 1*: I don't like watching the news, it is all about war and poor children being killed. What is happening to the children in Gaza is horrible.
*Girl 1*: It makes me very sad, you see blood everywhere, children's remains are scattered across the streets.
*Nisrine*: So, who is fighting in Gaza?
*Boy 2*: It is the rebels against the regime.
(Creative Workshop 4, Casablanca, July 2014)

While children were exposed to the news of Gaza around the clock, their engagement and understanding of the conflict reflected a minimal understanding of political affairs that might be typical of their age. However, this was not marginal viewing. Children were intensively exposed to the news on Gaza for most of the day and throughout the 40-day duration of the offensive. This suggests that unintentional exposure to the TV did not bring in-depth engagement with the content. Rather, it stirred feelings of identification with a universal condition of injustice towards children rather than a particular interest in the specificities of one conflict (Image 4.3).

In contrast, children in Morocco showed detailed and keen interest in content accessed through other platforms available to them. They were much more enthused by their adventures at the *Cyber* and the array of media activities they could do there—from films, to games, to social media. It was their own medial territory giving them ultimate freedom for choosing media content.

In Lebanon, children were the least tuned to the TV and used it as a last resort. When asked about their TV viewing habits, children in ethnographic visits and creative workshops expressed similar opinions:

*Nisrine*: In general, when do you watch TV the most?
*Lina*: When I am bored, and no one is talking to me
*Nisrine*: In general, is it in the mornings or afternoons?
*Lina*: Now for example [afternoon], in the morning I don't watch they put stuff for children.
*Nisrine*: in the evening?
*Lina*: if mum and dad are not watching I watch

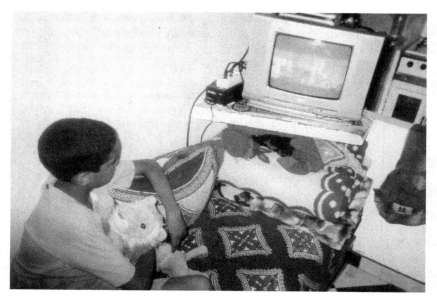

**Image 4.3**  Image of a TV set in the home of a low-income respondent in Casablanca. Permission granted as part of the research material

*Nisrine*: if mum and dad are watching do you sit with them to watch?
*Lina*: It's boring what they watch so I use mum's phone
*Nisrine*: you don't watch the stuff they watch, or do you watch a little bit?
*Lina*: they follow series, they are boring!
(Ethnography 9, Beirut, August 2015)
*Nisrine*: When do you watch TV?
*Suhail*: once I get bored
*Nisrine*: Throughout the day?
*Suhail*: I use the Ipad for games (clash of clans) and Youtube. Once I get bored I watch TV
(Creative workshop 9, August 2015)

Children's media use was clearly more dynamic than the availability of the TV would suggest. They hopped across platforms and devices, resorting to an array of activities beyond the rigidity of scheduled content and family viewing (Image 4.4).

**Image 4.4**  'My Life as Me' a drawing by an 11-year-old Lebanese girl living in Dubai

### Prime Object of Affection: The Phone and Socio-Material Presence

Across the three sites, one device transcended the socio-economic and spatial divides and occupied centre-stage in children's everyday lives. Phones were the most commonly available device at hand, at home, and outside of it. Parents had their own phones, as did older siblings. Some children had their own phones, while others were keenly awaiting the day their parents would allow them to have one. Parents in London and Beirut restricted phone acquisition for their children until they reached the ages of 10–12, while in Morocco, it was related more to the purchase power of the family.[2]

The phone appealed to children as part of an aesthetic–functional–affective object that intimately spoke of their personal style. When asked about her phone, Arwa, a 12-year-old Londoner, donned a big smile and her eyes sparkled as she held it close to her heart: "Ohhhhh I love it, love it love it. It has everything. I got a new cover for it. Look, it is pink with diamonds and a little cat on the side. It is so cute" (Ethnography 4, London, July 2013).

When asked what attracted them to the phone, children expressed their fondness in terms of materiality, portability, and functionality. The phone also shone over other devices, in that it combined unparalleled multifunctionality with intimacy and privacy:

> *Salwa*: [I prefer the] IPhone because on TV or computer you have to wait for it to come on. On the iPhone you put your password and it comes on. It's small and you can carry along. You can't carry a laptop with you. You can call on it as well, and text. I haven't got my own iPhone. When I am in year 7 I will get it.
> *Tarik*: What do you like most? The way they look? What you can do with them?
> *Salwa*: What I can do with them.
>
> (Creative Workshop 1, London, July 2013)

The keen affinity to the phone was echoed in Morocco and Lebanon. In particular, girls favoured the phone primarily for an array of functions. In her viewing diary, Nadia, a 10-year-old girl in the suburb of Casablanca, noted: "In the morning I turned on TV and watched Tom and Jerry cartons in Toyor El Iraq channel. At noon time I took mum's phone and played a Barbie game" (Ethnography 7, Casablanca, July 2014). Nadia explained that she resorts to the phone several times during the day, as a stop in between other group activities with her family and neighbouring friends at the *Derb*. For her, using the phone was a personal activity that she cherished dearly.

In Lebanon, Yasmin explained a similar use for her mom's phone:

> *Nisrine*: What do you like most phone or tablet?
> *Yasmin*: I dunno. I feel that the tablet is big, and you cannot talk using it.
> *Nisrine*: You prefer to talk?
> *Yasmin*: Yes, I use it for WhatsApp with my friends.
> *Nisrine*: Do you play any games on the phone?
> *Yasmin*: Oh yes, there are several. Look at this one, it is my favourite. You take a picture of yourself and then you can do anything to it—you can put make up on, change your hairstyle and colour. Let me take a photo of you and show you...
>
> (Ethnography 10, Beirut, August 2015)

In the most deprived households such as out-of-school Syrian refugee children in Lebanon, the phone had the most presence as both an entertainment and lifeline support device. Maimoun and his siblings' connectivity was more than restricted. His family had an old TV that only captured national non-satellite channels but had to sell it to make use of the money. His parents use their mobile phones as the main and only media devices available in the household. These were low tech smart phones, topped up with pay-as-you go credit for voice call minutes, texts, and data. The mobile phone turned out to be vital for both parents and children. It was a one-stop device that parents used to check on their loved ones through WhatsApp, Viber, and Facebook. They also received regular updates about their cash allowances from humanitarian providers. They also followed flash news on the war in Syria and watched regular entertainment like Syrian series or talent shows.

Maimoun and his siblings often borrowed their parents' phones throughout the day to browse the net (Ethnography 11, Beirut, August 2015). They were mostly home bound after they dropped out of school three years prior to the fieldwork, with Maimoun working full-time at a welding workshop to help with the household expenses. Maimoun and his siblings were among 300,000 other Syrian refugee children who are missing out on education in Lebanon (Watkins 2013). Being out of school, the children lost most of their literacy skills and they could hardly write down their names. Maimoun made dextrous use of digital technology to overcome his eroded literacy. Instead of the lengthy process of typing the search in the address bar, he quickly dictated his media choices, in his soft voice, and with his Syrian accent, to the voice search feature embedded in major platforms such as google and YouTube. Once on the net, Maimoun enjoyed watching exciting music video clips, cartoons, series, and variety shows—mostly Syrian productions—and playing internet games such as Super Mario.

## Conclusion

As the research unfolded over the three years, capturing average media use among Arabic-speaking children proved a delightfully elusive feat. The ethnography allowed us to venture into the manifolds of children's worlds as much as they and their parents allowed us to, of course. We were turning stones, manifesting interest in their daily lives, viewing habits, and preferences in an experimental and unusual way for us and for them. Throughout these explorations, the intangible mediated familiar of their everyday turned into a documented unfamiliar, allowing us and them to explore more folds to their worlds that we could not have otherwise captured.

The temporalities involved in children's media use outside of the school/summer break dichotomy were explored. In spite of the significantly reduced media time during the school term, this minimal amount was sufficient to keep children in tune with media trends across the year, with hardly any disconnect between winter and summer times. Their media use was more regular and fluid than we envisaged. Similarly, during the summer break, children's pastimes were more varied than the blanket 'optimal summer use' of the initial research design. As children diligently noted down in diaries and shared their activities with us, they revealed spatial and temporal variations, creating 'bracketed time-space happenings' within summer time that shaped their world-making processes. It is worth noting that children belonging to migrant households experienced the deepest bracketing of time during their summer breaks compared to their habitual media use during school time. However, it is also imperative to account for the fluidity of temporalities, spatialities, and socialities involved in non-migrant children's media use.

Children's usual social spaces also constituted networks of mediated socialities that formed children's worlds. Tracing these mediations opened up the analysis to imagine a multidimensional web-like network of connections that children moved across. The immediate social spaces in which children interacted also gave a fuller picture on the manifestations of identity formation. Across the three sites, significant spaces varied from the school (London), the *Derb* or neighbourhood (Casablanca), and the extended family (Beirut).

The home was the central stop where children spent chunks of 'in' time in between their summer busy schedules. From a crude socio-economic lens, the household's economic situation was obviously a determining factor in the array of media devices and platforms available for media access and use. However, the spatial organisation of the household and living arrangements significantly altered children's media use across socio-economic classes. Similarly, the negotiation of hierarchies within the family, mainly in relation to parents' pedagogic, cultural, and political ideals also affected what media reached children and how it was controlled. However, these negotiations have long departed from the early research focused on the TV as primary communal device of media uses and which is still dominant in epistemologies on Arabic-speaking children today.

Turning to the children's everyday schedules helped to reassess the hierarchy of media use and destabilise the centrality of the TV as the omnipresent medium of use. Children used different media to watch, play, and connect. They hopped between devices and platforms widening the scope of what is meant by media use from strict 'edutainment viewing' to complex assemblages of communicability that included watching programmes, playing games, and socialising through social media. The practices of children did not conform to the model of conversion. Children engaged in processes of bricolage of content, with variations in their affective engagement with different media and devices.

The phone came out as a coveted medium that children identified closely with and used eagerly in home and diasporic settings, bringing them on par with other children groups in Western settings (see Ofcom 2017). The phone transcended availability and ownership to presence. Regardless of their availability, children considered phones as among their most prized objects they used or possessed. It occupied children's imaginaries. From the most affluent to the poorest households, phones were in full presence. Across the three sites, children valued the phone as a marker of 'growing up'. Acquiring a phone was akin to a rite of passage that marked children's transition towards their independence from the cocooned middle years to their spirited teens. Children used the phone as a combined affective-epistemological act that was central to the many associative connections they held with their physical and social environment.

## NOTES

1. In Lebanon, the educational system includes state-run schools and private ones established mainly by religious authorities across the religious spectrum with a few exceptions. Since the civil war (1975–1990), state-run schools have been historically marginalised with lower state funding, untrained staff, overcrowded classes, and run-down facilities despite several attempts at reform since the 1990s.
2. In London, parents were in favour of getting phones for their children for safety reasons. As young as 10 years old, Londoner children enjoyed freedom of movement and used public transport to go to school and participate in other social activities and parents relied on the phone to check on them when they were out.

## Bibliography

Chatty, et al. (2014). *Ensuring Quality Education for Young Refugees from SYRIA (12–25 years): A Mapping Exercise* (Refugees Studies Centre Research Report) http://www.rsc.ox.ac.uk/files/publications/other/rr-syria-youth-education-2014.pdf.

Heidegger, M. (1962). *Being and Time.* London: Blackwell.

Hobsbawm, E. (1991). Exile. *Social Research, 58*(1), 67–68.

Keightley, E., & Pickering, M. (2012). *The Mnemonic Imagination: Remembering as Creative Practice.* London: Palgrave.

Latour, B. (2005). *Reassembling the Social: An Introduction to Actor-Network-Theory.* Oxford: Oxford University Press.

Morley, D. (2000). *Home Territories Media, Mobility and Identity.* London: Comedia.

Ofcom. (2017). *Children and Parents: Media Use and Attitudes Report.* www.ofcom.org.uk/_data/assets/pdf_file/0020/108182/children-parents-media-use-attitudes-2017.pdf.

Projansky, S. (2014). *Spectacular Girls: Media Fascination and Celebrity Culture.* New York: New York University Press.

Sabry, T. (2010). *Cultural Encounters in the Arab World: On the Media, the Modern and the Everyday.* London: I.B. Tauris.

Watkins, K. (2013). *Education Without Borders: A Summary: A Report from Lebanon on Syria's Out of School Children.* Overseas Development Institute.

### *Field Notes*

Creative Workshop 1, London, July 2013.
Creative Workshop 2, London, July 2013.
Creative Workshop 4, Casablanca, July 2014.
Creative Workshop 9, Beirut, August 2015.
Ethnography 1, London, July 2013.
Ethnography 2, London, July 2013.
Ethnography 3, London, July 2013.
Ethnography 4, London, July 2013.
Ethnography 5, Casablanca, July 2014.
Ethnography 6, Casablanca, July 2014.
Ethnography 7, Casablanca, July 2014.
Ethnography 9, Lebanon, August 2015.
Ethnography 10, Beirut, August 2015.
Ethnography 11, Beirut, August 2015.

CHAPTER 5

# Children, Media as '*Equipment*' and *Worldliness*

**Abstract** In this chapter, we make use of two further Heideggerian concepts—*worldliness* and *equipment*. We show, using evidence from fieldwork with children in the three sites of research, Casablanca, Beirut and London, how *Worldliness* postulates a distinctive structure. We explore *worldliness* as a totality in which media is but one constituent, among many, in the everyday lives of the children. We unpack, using different examples from ethnography, the ways in which media technology, and the communicative processes it instigates, can shape children's ontological experience of being-in-the-world. Thinking with and against Heidegger's phenomenological approach, we argue that a study of visible ontological phenomena in and by itself fails to capture the complexity of children's *worldliness*. While the children use the media texts intentionally for carving out 'mnemonic' and agential extensions of self, they also do so, we have observed, within hidden and unequal structures that put them at a disadvantage at the level of creativity, education, and other public service rights as young citizens.

**Keywords** Children · Worldliness · Technology · Equipment · Mnemonic · Being-in-the-world

T. Sabry and N. Mansour, *Children and Screen Media in Changing Arab Contexts*, https://doi.org/10.1007/978-3-030-04321-6_5

## INTRODUCTION

Someya escorted us through the narrow streets of Casablanca's old *Medina* into an area known as the *Mellah*, a former Jewish quarter, to meet Saadia and her sons: Marwan 12 and Omar 10. Someya is *Bnt Derb*, a phrase commonly used in Moroccan working-class popular cultural talk (literally meaning the daughter of the quarter) to refer to a female belonging to a certain quarter and who is also deserving of respect and protection, should any harm come to her. Someya greeted several people as we walked towards the old *Mellah*, the avant-garde of Casablancan subculture, slang, popular jokes, great footballers, and legendary burners who left the port of Casablanca illegally for different European cities armed only with *Meeka* (popular talk for plastic bag containing nuts and some water). The *Mellah* is also known for its veg and meat souk, especially its fresh and reasonably priced fish; second hand books and *kmaya* (hashish).

We'd timed our family ethnography in Casablanca in late July, just as we did in London and Beirut, to coincide with the summer school holidays. We walked *en route* to Saadia's house readied with our colourful 40-page holiday media diaries for the children, which we had written in the standard Arabic language as well as drawing and recording material. Someya finally stopped by a door, which was left wide open, and called out '*Salam Alaikum*' (Peace be upon you), a phrase also used to declare a guest's arrival. Saadia emerged out of a curtain, draped right before the entrance, which we later learnt separated the toilet from the rest of the room—the only room. Saadia's larger than life smile; her incessant and profusely welcoming words '*marhba marhba marhba*', welcomed us into her humble abode: a compact 3 × 3 metres room, including three small Moroccan sofas, a table, a cooking space, a fridge, a radio and a small working area with a sewing machine. A small television hung out of the wall, which was painted in the cheapest form of paint in Morocco known as *al-Jeer*. The Al-Jazeera live news coverage, *Gaza Resists*, reporting on the 2014 Israeli bombing of Gaza, was on.

The father, a tall bearded man who bore the hallmarks of a devout Muslim, and to whom we were only introduced briefly, had been out of a job for several years. Saadia was the main bread winner with the occasional sewing jobs she did from home. Saadia took great pride in her boys; they were both at primary school and doing well, especially the eldest Marwan. But Saadia had major concerns for her sons' future.

Their dire financial situation aside, the area they live in is notorious for drug use, delinquency, and high crime levels. These shortcomings were made the more conspicuous with the absence of public services and the indifference of the Moroccan state to the plight of the Moroccan poor working classes. Our design of the diary centred around children's school holidays. We had intentionally devised questions to capture the children's everyday lives, including: environment, media uses, playing with friends, and other activities. Omar and Marwan lived no more than 10 minutes' walk from the beach; yet, in all the three weeks we visited them, they barely went for an outing to the seaside.

*Worldliness* presupposes a distinctive structure in the way it un-conceals itself as such: the world—a world. But this distinctiveness as un-concealment can only come forth through *Dasein* or in our case: *the experiences of the ethnographic subject*. We were keen to understand how Omar and Marwan's *worldliness*—their universe—was conceived by them as a totality of objects. This phenomenological exercise—or the coupling of ethnographic observation with and through a phenomenological approach speaks directly to and is informed by our non-media-centric approach to the study of children and the media. In borrowing the Heideggerian concept *worldliness*, our aims are to explore *worldliness* as a totality in which media is a constituent. However, we were also keen to examine whether and how media may act, not merely as parts of a distinctive whole, but also as dynamic extensions of *worldliness*. Our focus in this study is on the ways in which media technology and the communicative processes it instigates can, alongside other phenomena, shape children's ontological experience of being-in-the-world. We are interested in the total system of *equipment* and practices which gives sense to the child's *worldliness*. To use Scannell's words, we are interested in the children's being-in-the-world, as opposed to being in one's head (Scannell 2014: 19). We are concerned with *worldliness* as outwardness rather than inwardness. This kind of *worldliness* comes more conspicuously to the fore in its shared-ness, in it being concernful and part of a social everyday world. It is a being-in-the world *with*.

> The being of entities which we encounter as closest to us can be exhibited phenomenologically if we take as our clue our everyday Being-in-the-world, which we also call our "dealings"[1] in the world and with entities within-the world. Such dealings have already dispersed themselves into manifold ways of concern. The kind of dealing which is closest to us is

as we have shown, not a bare conceptual cognition, but rather that kind of concern which manipulates things and puts them to use; and this has its own kind of knowledge. The phenomenological question applies in the first instance to the being of those entities which we encounter in such concern. (Heidegger 1962: 95)

Marwan's concern with the lack of an ethical public vision in his neighbourhood regarding health, education, and security comes out of a shared rather than a private experience. 'The world within which ... beings are encountered, is ... always already [a] world which one shares with the others' (Heidegger BP, 297, in Dreyfus 1991: 90). We see media, in a Heideggerian sense, as equipment.[2] Its function (uses), that of encountering (be it through voice, image or text), we argue, is the pre-existing care-structure which enables Omar and Marwan's worlds to extend beyond the confines of their $3 \times 3$ compact dwelling. The mobile phone, the radio programme, the television protruding from the wall, and the video-game are *the equipment* through the *uses* of which both the spatial the temporal and the imagination are extended. Uses of such *equipment* bring with it the unintentional possibility of being part of a more expansive *worldliness*—'a for-the-sake of which' and an 'in-order-to' structures. *Dasein*, advances Heidegger, 'finds "itself" primarily in what it does, uses, expects, avoids—in the environmentality available with which it is primarily concerned' (Heidegger [155] [119], in Dreyfus 1991: 96). In this case, and to follow on from Heidegger's definition of *worldliness*, media as ontic equipment are an apriori "entity", which we must discover in their "where-in" and *availableness* as a form of disclosure. We are keen to emphasise the usability and functionality of media as *equipment* for the children. '*Equipment*' observed Heidegger in *Being and Time*, 'is essentially something "in-order-to"... A totality of equipment is constituted by various ways of the "in-order-to", such as serviceability, conduciveness, usability and manipulability' (1962: 970). How do the media fit with other forms of the equipment-whole (*Zeugganzes*) and children's involvement-whole (*bewandtnisganzheit*)? We use Heideggerian concepts: "for-the-sake of-which" and "in-order-to" in the context of Omar and Marwan's uses of digital media technology, as both unintentional and intentional processes. But both these two intentionalities, we argue, lead to a significant purpose: carving out (*disclosing* and *discovering*) new spatio-temporal geographies of being and encountering that transcend the alienating confinements of materiality. A key question for us has been: How do we un-conceal the parts of the whole that make up the children's *worldliness* and what role do the media as *equipment* play in this process?

## CONTENT OF A TWO-WEEK MEDIA USE DIARY: MARWAN AND OMAR/CASABLANCA

| Programme | Language | Channel | Genre/uses |
|---|---|---|---|
| Dakar-Fez express: Enigma Tahaddi | Arabic | MEDI 1TV | Adventure/travel/competition |
| The amazing world of Gumball | Dubbed into Arabic from English | Cartoon network | Cartoons |
| Facebook | French/Arabic/Moroccan Arabic | Internet | Chat/Moroccans abroad/trans-national connectivity |
| Video games | French/English | Internet (café) | Video Games/internet (café) |
| Google | French/English | Internet | Games/music videos |
| Tom and Jerry | Dubbed into standard Arabic | Cartoon network/satellite | Cartoons |
| Uncle grandpa | Dubbed into standard Arabic | Cartoon network/satellite | Cartoons |
| Lu3batu al-hub (the game of love) | Turkish/dubbed into Moroccan Arabic | Moroccan TV1 | Drama |
| The transformers | English | Internet | Video game |
| News | Arabic | Al-Jazeera | Gaza war/news (Home) On most of the day/negotiating what to watch |
| Ben 10 | Dubbed into Arabic (English) | Cartoon network | Cartoons |
| Play football | English | Internet | Video games/internet café |
| Play formula | English | Internet | Video games/internet café |
| Top Span/Tennis | English | Internet | Video games/internet café |
| Attadawi Bela'shaab | Moroccan Arabic | Radio/Mediterranean FM | Radio talk/listening with mum |
| Yahya Angelo (Angelo Rules) | Dubbed into Arabic (English) | Cartoon network | Cartoons |
| Atfal wa bass | | MBC 3 | |

(continued)

(continued)

| Programme | Language | Channel | Genre/uses |
|---|---|---|---|
| Horror movies | Subtitled | MBC3 | Movies |
| Tahaddi al-Abtaal | Arabic | MBC3 | |
| Waadi adeaab | Dubbed from Turkish into Moroccan Arabic | Nasma?/Turkish | Drama |
| Hdiddan | Moroccan Arabic | 2 M | Comedy/Moroccan folk culture/story telling |
| Haha wa tufaha | Egyptian | 2 M | Egyptian film |
| Bollywood movies | Subtitled | MBC bollywood | Films/love the music/dance/ stories |
| Action movies | Subtitled | MBC action | Films/no parental guidance |
| Qessat alnass (stories of people) | Moroccan Arabic | MEDI 1 TV | Talk shows: social issues |

The summary of Marwan and Omar's media uses over a period of two weeks brings a number of issues to the fore. Our diaries were designed to help us learn about the viewing habits and media uses of Arab children in different parts of three cities: London, Beirut, and Casablanca. A key intentional aim was to learn how children's media uses in these three sites are embedded within children's structures of everyday life. In the case of Omar and Marwan, for us to unpack processes of *disclosing* and those of *discovering*, uses of the media as *equipment* had to be read within the context of their everyday life. Diclosedness manifests itself in the care-structure built into several programming (Moroccan or foreign) and in its character of laying open a universe with which the children became familiar. Their being-in-the-world extends beyond their material reality to un-conceal being in the world as 'skilled activity'. We were very impressed with the technical ease and familiarity with which Omar and Marwan navigated between different digital media, including participation in social media platforms, negotiating viewing and media use time (see Morley 1992: 175), and using different search engines in different languages to download and view material.

In the morning, I watch cartoons like Gumball in the Cartoon Network. In the afternoon I go to the cybercafé to chat in Facebook … I have 988 friends from different countries. I also log into play websites.

(Ethnography 5, Casablanca, July 2014)

Media as *equipment* had also disclosed rich cultural encounters with pro-gramming from Turkey, The US, Europe, Egypt, India, the UK, Qatar, Saudi Arabia, and Latin America. Processes of *disclosing* and *discovery* had led to technical and cultural familiarity resulting in a *worldliness* sel-dom ascribed to the poor working classes in media studies and sociology. This is because the dominant discourse in both disciplines often privi-leges hermeneutics of suspicion as a default position for thinking about media and their audiences. A media studies that is unable to think out-side the hermeneutics of suspicion, as a default position, is also by default un-reflexive since it cannot imagine what lies outside it or its ideologi-cal positioning. This also raises questions about the sociological catego-ries we often take for granted in our writing and analyses which tend to unreflexively frame experience within rigid categories. It is no exaggera-tion to confirm that we had found Omar and Marwan's experiences of *worldliness*—its diclosedness and availableness—to be richer than that of some children we interviewed in London and others from middle-class backgrounds in Beirut and Casablanca. Having access to a rich and var-ied media content is usually prescribed to the middle classes and never to the poor working classes whose uses of the media are often studied within the politics of marginality, alienation, and dysfunctionality. In our attempt to un-conceal the children's *worldliness* and their media uses, we opted for a phenomenological approach, with the focus on things as they are; as they reveal themselves to us, as opposed to something that is in our head.

> Phenomenology is firmly committed to a view that thinking begins by looking outwards rather than inwards. In an originary sense we are moved (summoned) to thinking by looking at the world, the alpha and Omega of all thought – where thinking begins and ends. The point is not to contem-plate the world, still less to presume to change it – but perhaps, at least, to recognize, acknowledge and try to understand it. This is what phenome-nology essays. (Scannell 2014: 5)

Omar and Marwan were more in tune with local issues. Saadia, their mother, has favourite television programmes which she watches reli-giously with her children. A popular television talk show they watch fre-quently on Midi1TV is *Quessat Nass* (people stories). The programme, broadcast in Moroccan Arabic, engages its audiences with key social issues including; divorce, rape, drug use, crime, etc. The host of the talk show invites people to the programme, usually people to whom a grave injustice is done, who then are able to tell their stories in front of a studio audience. Watching the programme almost 5 times a week discloses a local world for Omar and Marwan with which they are already familiar and is part of their everyday experience. Saadia had serious concerns for the safety of her children because of the high levels of crime in their area, usually induced by drug use. Saadia uses people's stories in the programme to engage her children with consequences of drug use. They also discuss other social issues such as the poor standards of public health care in state hospitals. The programme, mainly popular with children from working-class backgrounds, discloses a type of publicness (giving ordinary, usually working-class people a platform to tell their stories on television) that is unavailable to the middle-class children in Casablanca who did not watch the programme. Omar and Marwan also listened (with their mother) to a range of talk radio programmes, including programmes on alternative medicine (Image 5.1).

**Image 5.1** Drawing of a 12-year-old boy in Casablanca noting his aspirations to 'build hospitals and dispensaries, be fair and not deceitful, be a famous footballer, do a great job and reach a high position in society'. Permission granted as part of the research material

I wish also that the situation of the Moroccan citizen would change and be better because wherever you go you face struggles and challenges. For example, when you go to the public hospital, they don't let the doctor see you at the time, they tell you to return in another time which means that if you want to die just do it nothing would change. Then the only solution you have is that you have to go to the private hospital and pay money in order to see the doctor. If you want to see the doctor in the public hospital you have to give money too, although its services are for free.

(Ethnography 5, Casablanca, August 2014)

One of Omar and Marwan's favourite Moroccan programmes on television is *Enigma Tahadi*, an adventure programme involving contestants (mostly adults) from different parts of Morocco, who are set physical and mental challenges, filmed in several parts of Morocco and showcasing the country's great landscapes and touristic attractions.

> *Enigma Tahadi* is a nice and beneficial programme from which we learn a lot. Most of its programmes are filmed in historical and fascinating places in Morocco.
>
> (Ethnography 5, Casablanca, July 2014)

Omar and Marwan's being in the world is predetermined by a process of dual-diclosedness; their immediate environment, the 3 × 3 metres home and their mother, father, and other family entourage in Casablanca. We can also add the school, the street, the shops, the Internet café, and the mosque. The other form of diclosedness is mediated through ontic *equipment* that both anchors their localised experiences and extends their being to other forms of *worldliness*—in this case, a diclosedness that brings Morocco with all its stunning views and landscapes to their run-down, badly ventilated, and windowless 3 × 3 metres home. Here, being-in-the-world is predetermined by a process of constant coping that media as *equipment* make not only possible but also familiar. *Enigma Atahdi*, a programme of adventure, is a travelling vehicle that compensates for the boys' immobility. It has made it possible for them to travel to parts of Morocco they would not otherwise have been able to experience. It has thus stretched their spatial *worldliness* without the confines of immediate and physical materiality. Marwan and Omar support Barcelona, dance to Rai music, sing along to Bollywood movies, get excited by Hollywood action, watch mum cry watching Turkish soap, play Japanese video games, travel in Morocco virtually through *Tahadi Enigma*. What this confers is reminiscent of Raymond Williams's unexampled mobility '...it is not living in a cut-off way, not in a shell that is stuck. It is a shell which you can take with you' (1989: 171). But mobility in the cases of Omar and Marwan is not merely spatial; it is also psychic and temporal.

Exposure to daily news coverage via the Qatari channel Aljazeera, especially during Israel's bombing of Gaza in 2014 meant that both Omar and Marwan had, like many children around the globe who are increasingly witnessing war violence on television news (see Lemish and Götz 2007), consumed hours of explicit news coverage from Gaza with graphic images of death, especially of children. Since everyone lived in just the one room, coverage of death and destruction was unavoidable. Omar and Marwan spoke with sadness about the plight of Gazans and have especially empathised with the many children who died or were injured during the conflict:

> They are really suffering. Small children, young and old die without any justification. The Israeli army attacks innocent civilians. They kill people and damage everything that is Palestinian. Netanyahu and Sisi are torturing Palestinians.
>
> (Ethnography 5, Casablanca, July 2014)

## WORLDLINESS AS IMAGINATION

Throughout out the ethnographic study, we asked children from the three different sites: Beirut, Casablanca, and London, to talk to us about their aspirations for the future. The question: "what do you want to be when you grow up?" was repeated across our three methods: family interview, holiday diary, and the creative workshop. This is not an uncommon line of questioning. Children are usually asked this question by their family members, and in other contexts, think for example of the live children TV shows where such a question is pretty much the life line of ordinary everyday talk. We built this question into our research design not to merely prompt a conversation with the children, but to see how they imagined themselves temporally in the world. We also wanted to find out what alternative world(s) were imagined by them in relation to their lived everyday experiences. When Marwan was asked what he wanted to be when he grew up, he did not hesitate:

> *Marwan*: I would like if I have money to establish an association of medicines and hospitality because a lot of people don't have money to buy medicines and to go to the hospital to cure them. This is my dream I want to achieve it in future.

*Tarik*: I see that the issue of hospitals matters a lot to you.
*Marwan's mum*: Yes, because we suffer with them [Moroccan state and private health] a lot, now we have a health card named Rami that helps people to go to the hospital and pay only half of what they should pay.
(Ethnography 5, Casablanca, July 2014)

Bayan, a 12-year-old Palestinian refugee girl from the Yarmouk Palestinian Camp in Syria, fled, in a double forced migration, to Chatila, the Palestinian Camp in the outskirts of Beirut. She tragically witnessed the murder of her father by a sniper as her family was trying to cross a checkpoint outside Yarmouk, and expressed her aspirations through drawing. And she too had imagined her being in the future in relation to her past and present experiencing of her *worldliness*:

*Bayan*: "Hello, how are you? I did some nice work with my friend that I'll show you right now. I felt here that I was a butterfly, a big red butterfly. My siblings are the small butterflies in yellow; these are my mum and dad. I am from Palestine. I didn't want to write a lot I wanted to express myself with drawings. This is a heart. I love watching TV especially MBC3. I love this channel. I am 12 years old. I love you a lot, a lot. This was in the past. Now I am telling you about the present. I am not a big red butterfly anymore, I am a green small green butterfly. I am here Bayan, but I live in Syria. I am still Palestinian but now I am in Lebanon. I love mathematics and science. I like to watch *Baraem* (children's programme), MBC3, Cartoon Network. At first, I loved MBC 3 only but then I discovered the other two. Now I will speak about the future. The Future is beautiful; I didn't see it, but I will imagine it. I want to be an engineer".
*Nisrine*: Thank you. Applaud! I have a question; why do you want to be an engineer?
*Bayan*: So when I go back to Palestine, we will build it again.
(Creative workshop 8, Beirut, August 2015)

Bayan's imagined future is temporally ordered in her drawing according to past, present, and future. Bayan first recalls a worldliness from her past experience, perhaps as a refugee in Syria when she was happier. Bayan's identification with a big red butterfly in the past is juxtaposed with a transformation to a small green butterfly in the present. While we cannot deduce much at the level of connotation from comparing red and green butterflies, perhaps the two colours are connotative of different emotions. Perhaps red is connotative of a happier affective state than green.

But what is clear is that the change to a smaller butterfly in the present is suggestive of a metamorphosis to a less significant and a less important entity. In the past, Bayan felt loved and cared for. Red perhaps, without wanting to fix meaning within a west-centric context, is perhaps a connotation for love—for the love she felt for her family, mum and dad, and her yellow butterfly siblings. What is striking in Bayan's drawing is the inclusion of media as *equipment*—Bayan did not just like the channels she mentions; she loved them. Bayan declares her love for MBC3: "I Love you, I love you a lot". It is worth noting here how media form part of the totality of Bayan's worldliness, a worldliness which she clearly attributes to a past temporality, perhaps a happier past. Bayan's present-ness in the world, her being in the now of the interview and the work-shop is discursively juxtaposed for us to a past temporality to evoke change and transformation from one experience to another. The trans-formation from a big red butterfly to a small green butterfly is indicative of a different experience of being in the world. What we have insight into here is a whole affective regime of a 12-year-old child's exilic expe-rience, provoked by a double-displacement, marginalisation, and alien-ation. "I am here, Bayan, but I live in Syria. I am still Palestinian, but I live in Lebanon". Bayan's imagination of the future is anchored by a profound and short statement: "Now I will speak about the future. The Future is beautiful; I didn't see it, but I will imagine it. I want to be an engineer". Just as we saw with the Maimoun Family and with Marwan, the child from the Old medina of Casablanca, children defy the objective realities of their worldliness: a 'for-the-sake of which' and an 'in-order-to' structures come to the fore again. *Dasein*, in this case, finds "itself" not only in what 'it does, uses, expects, avoids—in the envi-ronmentality available with which it is primarily concerned', but also in what it imagines and what it defies; "the future is beautiful" speaks to the resourcefulness of many of the refugee children to whom we talked. These children cannot only imagine a beautiful future, a better world-liness, they also imagine their roles in this happier worldliness as fix-ers: Mahdi wants to sing to make people feel better, Marwan wants to become a doctor to help the poor who cannot get access to medicine or good health care, Bayan wants to become an engineer, so she can help rebuild Palestine. Although imagination is an inward rather than an out-ward phenomenon, I imagine a world in my head, a future; imagination is a *futuralness* that has yet to come, but which is both subjectively and objectively concerned with *worldliness* as it is lived in the now.

## THE ETHNOGRAPHER'S BODY AS TECHNICITY OF DISCOVERY

Nisrine Mansour, my co-researcher and the co-author of this book, is what I would call an avant-garde Arab academic, artist, and activist. Her 'trendy' hair-style and laid-back look made her an object of curiosity for many of the children we worked with in London, Beirut, and Casablanca. In Morocco, the combination of Nisrine's hairstyle and her Lebanese accent elevated her status from that of a mere ethnographer to that of a star. The children were curious about Nisrine's hairstyle—and when she spoke to them, they were star struck, as they associated her Arabic accent with that of the women they watch on Turkish, Lebanese, and Syrian television programmes. The girls especially wanted to know if Nisrine was married. For my part, I had no trendy hair-style to boast about, in fact I am bald. It was, however, my slightly darker complexion and my Moroccanness that made me the object of othering, especially with Lebanese children.

In one of the workshops in Casablanca, the following conversation took place between Nisrine and other children:

*Nisrine*: Do you have any questions you would like to ask me?
*Girl 1*: How old are you?
*G2*: 30? 40?
*Nisrine*: (smiles)
*G2*: You are 40? My mom is 40.
*Boy 1*: Where were you born?
*Nisrine*: Beirut, Lebanon.
*G3*: My friend is from Lebanon.
*G1*: Are you married?
*Nisrine*: No.
*G2*: Oh, my days! You are 40 and you are not married! My mom got married when she was 21.
*Nisrine*: why did you ask me these questions? Why was it important for you to know who I am?
*In group*: Coz you look young, pretty, and married.
*G2*: You look like you travel a lot and stuff.
*Nisrine*: How can you tell?
*G1*: I can tell from your hair.
*Tarik*: what can you tell from her hair?
*B1*: She is from a different country, and she has a smile on her face.

*G3*: Her experience, her accent. And the way she is acting. She is not acting.

*B3*: sometimes you can tell where you are from by your skin colour as well.

*B1*: You are very lucky you travelled. I have not travelled anywhere.

(Creative Workshop 2, London, July 2013)

The point in positioning the ethnographer's body and language as a form of available, outward worldliness is intentional. The children with whom we conversed and worked over the three-year period of the research were very adept at spotting difference. Their curiosity (and line of questioning, as we see above) is deeply rooted in what they perceived, even as young as 8, 9, and 10 years of age, as the socio-cultural norm. Social expectations are already set in: A woman at the age of 40 is expected to be married with children. What's quite revealing, however, is the association the children make between the ethnographer's look and worldliness. Nisrine's looks and behaviour disclose a different way of being in the world for the children. This form of othering as discovery, prompted by curiosity, was explained by the children as an advantage. Nisrine was seen as a 'worldly' person—a person who'd become different (looks), but wiser (behaviour) through travel and worldly encounters. Focusing on Nisrine's age also un-conceals how the children think about gender. I was not asked any questions about my age or my marital status, but Nisrine was because she is a woman. How Nisrine spoke, looked, and behaved were an object of curiosity for the children because she, for them, did not conform to what they thought was the social norm. In this context, the body and voice of the ethnographer (as the other) function as an *equipment* through which a kind of discovery about being different in the world is made. My position as an othered researcher/ethnographer was more pronounced whilst conducting ethnography with children in the Lebanon. My Moroccan accent and darker complexion were a giveaway. I can recall different instances when I felt totally othered by the children either because of race or language. This level of othering was more prominent when I worked with Armenian and Maronite Lebanese children. In an attempt to be comprehended by the children, I spoke in a standard Arabic rather than in a colloquial Lebanese Arabic. It was either this or use of my Moroccan Arabic which I did try but only through the request of my research partner to perhaps make a point. Arabs come in different shades. It was only after we had conducted ethnography in Morocco that I understood the reasons for my estrangement as an Arab. I am in the first place a Moroccan with Amazigh heritage. Standard Arabic was spoken in the house as a resistance to French and French imperialism. Arabic was, in this instance, more of a tool for me rather than part of a structure of feeling about the world. Arabness was and still is a construct, a teleological attempt at essentialising and authenticating experience. It is a farce. What came out of discussions with children in Morocco apropos their belonging and identity was revealing. When asked whether they identified with Islam, Moroccanness, or Arabness, Moroccan children did not hesitate to place Moroccanness and Islam ahead of Arabness at the level of identitarian identification. In fact, young Moroccan children did not identify much with Arabness as a structure of feeling. Being an Arab for them was cogently defined as a linguistic matter. For them, the Arabs are the Egyptians, the Lebanese, people living in the Gulf, the Syrians, etc. whose accents are too familiar because of Al-Jazeera news, Egyptian soap operas, Turkish drama (dubbed into Lebanese/Syrian dialects), and Lebanese singing competitions such as *Pop Idol*. Some of the Moroccan children were able to recite the Koran, sing popular Lebanese songs, and many of them have memorised many Arabic songs from the Jordanian-owned channel *Toyour al-Jannah*; Arab soundscapes are also prominent in markets and houses, ranging from Um Kalthoum, Abdel Haleem Hafez to the famous Egyptian Koran reciter Abdel Basset Assamad; yet, for these children, Arabic and Arabness constitute a less significant element in their *worldliness* and structure of feeling about the world. They defined themselves as being Moroccan first, then Muslim, and finally as Arabs. Arabic is for the children the language of the written word, the Koran and education. It is not their everyday language; Moroccan is. Moroccan *dareja* (colloquial accent) is more attuned to the hybrid postcolonial identity of Moroccan children, as it represents a whole repertoire of cultural encountering: Tamazight (Berber), Portuguese, Spanish, French, and Arabic. Just as in Abdelkabir Khatibi's *Tattooed Memory*, Moroccanness is inextricably linked to rich and complex cultural traits that transcend the rigid essentialisations of ideological demagogues: Moroccanness and Moroccan (though not a written language) speak to a more complex experience of belonging and being in the world. It is as if encounters with the other (the colonialist or 'charming' invader) had been tattooed onto the fabric of Moroccan identity. The children got it right: In Morocco, Arabness is not considered in the first place as a racial category; rather, it is strongly conceptualised from a linguistic perspective. But it is a language that is both sacred and profane; sacred because God speaks Arabic and profane because it is also the language of *Pop idol* and the MBC empire. As such, Arabness is not a key constituent of Moroccan children's worldliness; it is a mere part of its totality. Worldliness comes to the fore more visibly through structures of the everyday. Since Moroccan is the everyday language par excellence through which Moroccans converse, it becomes by default the *equipment* through which technologies of the self are delineated. The children impress upon Moroccan (language) the mark of its being as a language and a structure of feeling.

Our experience working with the Maimouns, a Syrian refugee family living in the Hezbollah-controlled area of Dahia, not far from the Palestinian camp Burj-al Barajneh, saw us positioned as 'others' and a source of discovery for the children with whom we conducted ethnography, beyond the tropes of race and language. In our introductory session, both Nisrine and I explained where we had come from and what the project entailed, etc. I did not expect on the mention of my nationality, *Moroccan*, to get an extended and, I have to add, intriguing introduction on Moroccans by the father, to which the children and their mother listened with fascination. Recalling an encounter with a Moroccan colleague back in the 1990s when he worked as a mechanic in Libya, Maimoun (the father) eloquently explained how Moroccans were known for *Sihr* (black magic): 'Moroccans have magical powers', the father added, 'they are masters at *sihr*. The father's story had elevated my presence in the eyes of the children with whom I was going to spend the next three weeks from that of a mere researcher to a magical *equipment*, a flying Sinbad, a source of mystery and excitement. The purpose of me recalling this episode from fieldwork is not accidental. It is an opening to the next section on Religion, Othering, and Worldliness. Also, the story was remarkably told by the head of the Maimoun family that had he told it before, its content may well have been the children's reference point for everything Moroccan. The story telling here is too an *equipment* through which other forms of worldliness make themselves available to the children. Remember that in the case of the Maimoun family, the television was a cadaver. It was storytelling, reminiscing about the past and mum's mobile phone through which the children's worldliness un-conceals itself.

## RELIGION, WORLD, AND OTHERS

In our attempt to unpack the role played by the media as *equipment*, we asked the children in all three sites to tell us what their favourite and less favourite countries were. The aim was not to test their geographic knowledge, but to assess how their immediate socio-cultural environment and the media as *equipment* of disclosure presented other counties to them. The extract below from a Morocco workshop in a working-class area of Casablanca delineates different forms of othering about those they see as others.

> *Tarik*: What are the countries you like and the countries you don't like?
>
> *Girl 1*: the country I like is Morocco because it is beautiful. And I don't like China because it is full of factories that pollute the weather and as a result it doesn't contain clean air.
>
> *Boy* 1: I like Morocco, Emirates, Saudi Arabia and China.
>
> *Nisrine*: why do you like the Emirates?
>
> *B1*: Because it includes exciting places like Khalifa Tower and that date tree designed inside the sea. I like Saudi Arabia because it is much organised.
>
> *B2*: I like Morocco because it is the most peaceful country I know.
>
> *Nisrine*: what are the countries that have war?
>
> *All*: PALESTINE, SYRIA, LYBIA
>
> *B3*: I don't like Iran because it is Shi'a and Shia's insult Islamic values.
>
> *G1*: Shia's are bad. They are people who worship the grandsons of our prophet pbh, and in '*Ashora* they hit themselves showing faith to Hassan and Hussein.
>
> *Nisrine*: how did you know this?
>
> *G1*: I've asked an Imam and he explained everything to me.
>
> *B2*: I hate Christians because they think that Jesus ('*Aissa*) is the son of Allah and this is not right.
>
> *Nisrine*: How do you know this?
>
> *All*: We watched it on TV.
>
> (Creative Workshop 5, Casablanca, July 2014)

On the whole, we found children from the working classes to be more exposed to tropes of cultural salafism than those from the middle classes. Cultural Salafism operates through the mediatic (television, radio, and mobile phones) and the social (the role of group leaders/family, friends, Friday prayer sermons) to transform a richly varied and moderate religious experience (which it describes as impure/innovation) with a more puritanical singular form of religiosity. Cultural Salafism and its preachers act by homogenising cultural and religious experience—their ultimate motif is masked by a pseudo-rationalism, the main aim of which is to de-metisise religious and cultural experience (Sabry 2019). Sunni Salafists see Shiism, Christianity, and Judaism as a deviation from the true religion. Only they, they purport, have the key the true and uncorrupted faith. This discourse is clearly seeping into social life in Morocco, especially in poor working-class areas. The evidence for this was clear in the working-class group workshops (see extract above) we conducted in Casablanca. Many of the children certainly saw Christianity, Judaism, and Shiism not only as an 'other', but also as corrupted and therefore illegitimate faiths. After some hesitation during this workshop, we prompted the children to tell us why they thought the way they did about Shiism, Judaism, and Christianity. The children were utterly surprised when we confirmed to them that most of the prophets in the Koran were Jewish including Moses and Jesus, that Mary, also a Jew, is revered in the Koran and by all Muslims. It was clear to us after this particular workshop that children were exposed to cultural salafism[3] in its socialised form. This is where cultural salafism is most potent as an ideology, when it is able to infiltrate everyday popular culture, the street corners, mosques, the Barber's shop, and other public everyday spaces. The children's reference to television as a source of knowledge about other religious faiths is equally important, for the socialised form of everyday, popular salafism is anchored by global religious channels, available through satellite media.

We asked a group of children from a middle-class quarter of Casablanca (including four girls and two boys) the same question. Their liberal upbringing and private French schooling reveal a different positioning on religion and Arabness.

> *Tarik*: What are the countries you love and the countries you don't?
> *Girl 1*: America and Europe because they are opened countries and I don't like Morocco and Arab countries.
> *G2*: I hate all the Arab countries because they are fanatics and close minded and full of conflicts … I prefer western countries.
> *G3*: It is Moroccan people who push you to emigrate because they judge you a lot, for example; once a woman is not veiled, she is automatically seen as decadent or something else.
>
> (Creative Workshop 6, Casablanca, August 2014)

The middle-class group was less interested in talking about religion. And when they did, they framed it within discourses of fundamentalism and terrorism. The girls in the group were especially vigorous in critiquing not one but all Arab countries, which they saw as a source of backwardness and religious fanaticism. Arabness for them connotes conflict, violence, and religious extremism. The West, on the other hand, is championed for its openness and respect for otherness. It is clear from this schism in framing the 'other', how habitus, education, environment, and the media play a fundamental role in shaping children's worldliness. Children are able to form ideas about the world in so far as ideas about the world become available to them. The children, as we saw in the cases of Marwan and Omar, are resourceful in carving out spatial and symbolic extensions, thanks to digital media, that transcend their objective material realities and they do this with utter skill and ingenuity. However, to argue with Heidegger in all of this that *worldliness* is a mere outward phenomenon is also to subscribe to a kind of hermeneutics that privileges care and trust at the expense of suspicion. It is also the type of hermeneutics that is more apt to dealing with visible rather than hidden phenomena. Where does this trust-outward-based thesis of *worldliness* leave us and our ethnography?

While the phenomenological method is hugely useful to the ethnographer in unpacking socio-cultural practices unhinged by predetermined theses or teleology, it leaves many questions unanswered. What the Heideggerian method misses is what is hidden in the things that make up the everyday in which we live. Un-concealing children's worldliness be they in the UK, in Morocco, or in Lebanon, its totality, we argue, is the product of both visible and hidden things—the study the technologised world of everyday things, equipment, discovery, the outward phenomenological world of the children we worked with is, we argue, insufficient as a methodology to provide a 'thick description', for unpacking children's worldliness. Heidegger himself had insisted in *Being and Time* that the world is complex because it both conceals and un-conceals itself for us. Phenomenology is more useful as a method when it is deployed to un-conceal not only the 'care-structures' that make our world work, but also the hidden things (structures) that produce and reproduce our everyday environment. Yes, children's worldliness is a product of availableness, performativity, affect, and discovery, but underlying this worldliness are hidden historical dimensions that too need un-concealing. Hermeneutics of trust and those of suspicion should not necessarily cancel each other out (see Scannell 2014). Children's *worldliness* in Morocco, regardless of the resourcefulness of the poor, is structurally divided into haves and have nots. Their worldliness conceals inequalities in care, in education, and in accessing modernity's objects of desire. Children's worldliness in Beirut conceals a structural violence and sectarianism that had made 'othering' into a respectable sport. The children's worldliness is also subject to a ruthless neo-liberal system which has privatised different aspects of every-day life, including care, education, employment, even beaches. These are the hidden structures of the world—children's world—that a merely out-ward looking phenomenology cannot tackle. Phenomenological un-con-cealment must adopt both hermeneutics of trust and hermeneutics of suspicion if it is to come to terms with the complexity of the world, and in our case, the children's worldliness. As ethnographers, we rehearsed how to observe and construct reality at the same time. This epistemic task is the product of an interpellation (a double-take) between the affec-tive register that comes with the encounter of the face of the other, the trodden, the robbed, the hopeful, and the stabilising of hermeneutics that takes place at the level of the institution: the academic institution. The worldliness we grappled with was, in the first instance, performed for us. Children's worldliness is affective. Not because they are children, but because they performed being-in their world for us, which affected us. They sang, they danced, they joked, they showed us how to play their video games, and they asked difficult questions. We observed their real-ities and were affectively involved in the process. The phenomenological method must un-conceal both visible and hidden phenomena. It is after all visibility and hiddenness that characterise the world. The decision to use a phenomenological method was driven by an interest in unpacking childhood outside the transcendent concepts used by sociology, psychol-ogy, and media studies to engage with the relationship between children and the media. Phenomenology facilitates a non-media-centric media stud-ies. This method has also allowed us a necessary epistemic manoeuvre: to de-territorialise (think outside sociology's hermeneutics) in order to re-ter-ritorialise (reconnect with sociology, particularly with its hermeneutics of suspicion). A 'non-media-centric' *children and the media* approach is necessary if we are to un-conceal perhaps other mediatic objects/things/ phenomena/contexts where screen, technology, face, the broken TV, the body, and where a multiplicity of registers merge in a totality. Digital media and their uses are an everyday thing, children go about the world digitally because of the availableness and familiarity of this world for them.

Digitality is just a worldly human thing. It is a way of being-in. We can certainly speak of a digital way of life that extends beyond the confines of technology onto the popular, the conversational, the affective, and the cultural. The problem, however, in fetishising digitality beyond the cultural practices it produces, is that it risks undermining the contexts in which the digital world unfolds for the children. This chapter has attempted to engage with children's media uses as 'equipment' which in turn plays, as we tried to show, a role in structuring not only the children's everyday lives, but also their formed ideas of the world (*worldliness*). We are conscious, in this chapter as in this whole book, that an understanding of Arab children's *worldliness* and its relation to media as *equipment* also necessitates, as Kerstin Pike rightly argues (2018), an exploration of the ways in which Arab children negotiate the 'merging, and blurring of boundaries between, local/Arab Gulf and global/US [media] content' (p. 80).

## NOTES

1. The translators of this edition of *Being and Time*—John Macquarrie and Edward Robinson—opted for "dealings" as a translation for the German word *Umgang*. In their footnote of the same page 95, they also give other possible translations. The word literally means 'going about', as in 'going about' one's business. We find the latter literal explanation to be more suited to the way we engage with the term later in the chapter.
2. *Equipment* is a translation for the German word '*das Zeug*'. According to Macquarrie and Robinson, the translators of *Being and Time* (1962, Blackwell), *Zeug* has no precise English equivalent. According to them: 'Heidegger uses it for the most part as a collective noun to our relatively specific "gear" … or the still more general "equipment"', a word they use throughout to denote *Zeug* (1962: 97).
3. A puritanical form of Islam that draws inspiration from the time of the Prophet Mohammed and his companions.

## BIBLIOGRAPHY

Bird, S. E. (2003). *The Audience in Everyday Life*. London: Routledge.
Bird Rose, D. (1996). *Nourishing Terrains: Australian Aboriginal Views of Landscape and Wilderness*. Canberra: Australian Heritage Commission.
Dreyfus, L. H. (1991). *Being-in-the World: A Commentary on Heidegger's Being and Time Division 1*. London: MIT Press.
Heidegger, M. (1962). *Being and Time*. London: Blackwell.

Heidegger, M. (1992). *The Concept of Time: The First Draft of Being and Time.* London: Continuum.

Lemish, D., & Götz, M. (Eds.). (2007). *Children and Media in Times of Conflict and War.* Cresskill, NJ: Hampton Press.

Morley, D. (1992). *Television Audiences and Cultural Studies.* London: Routledge.

Pike, Kerstin. (2018). Disney in Doha Arab Girls Negotiate Global and Local Versions of Disney Media. *The Middle East Journal of Culture and Communication, 11*(1), 72–90.

Sabry, T. (2019). Cultural Time and Everyday Life in the Middle Atlas Mountain Village of Ait Nuh. In Sabry & Khalil (Eds.), *Culture, Time and Publics in the Arab World.* London: I.B. Tauris.

Scannell, P. (2014). *Television and the Meaning of the Live. An Enquiry into the Human Situation.* Cambridge: Polity Press.

Williams, R. (1989). *Resources of Hope: Culture, Democracy, Socialism.* London: Verso.

## FIELD NOTES

Creative Workshop 2, London, July 2013.
Creative Workshop 5, Casablanca, July 2014.
Creative Workshop 6, Casablanca, August 2014.
Creative workshop 8, Beirut, August 2015.
Ethnography 5, Casablanca, July 2014.

CHAPTER 6

# Conclusion

**Abstract** The conclusion of this volume distils the main conceptual and methodological articulations emerging from the research. It reconciles the Heideggerian concept of 'thrownness' with reflexive ethnography to articulate the situatedness of the researcher in the field. It also elaborates on the ethnographic research *process* that, in and by itself, is worthy of systematic critique and reflection. This process un-conceals a more complex structure that fuses the affective, the empirical, the ethical, and the existential. The chapter then turns to the ethnographic evidence which points to a clear disjunction between 'Arabness' as a discursive, pan-Arabist narrative and 'Arabness' as a structure of feeling about the world. The ethnographic research uncovered varied and complex media uses by the children in the three sites. Again, Heidegger's concept 'equipment' was borrowed to unpack children's media uses because, as a concept, it captured the functional ways in which the children used the media that enabled them to extend beyond the confines of their material realities.

**Keywords** Arabness · Ethnography · Equipment · Process · Phenomenology · Heidegger · Method · Thrownness · Technicity · Performative

T. Sabry and N. Mansour, *Children and Screen Media in Changing Arab Contexts*, https://doi.org/10.1007/978-3-030-04321-6_6

## On Method

We borrowed the Heideggerian concept 'throwness' and applied it to our reflexive ethnography because it captured, for us, like no other concept, the situatedness of the researcher in the field who has to (a) grapple not only with childhood both as an ontological and as an epistemological category, but also with (b) spatial and temporal thrownness. In both cases, this made it critically important for us to engage in a systemic reflection on the *process* of our research. We emphasise *process* rather than findings for it had become apparent to us right from the start that process was, in and by itself worthy of systematic critique and reflection, for rather than it being merely about method, process un-conceals a more complex structure that fuses in the case of our ethnography; the affective, the empirical, the ethical and the existential. As such and as we observed in this book, *thrownness* is an existential condition that is at once traversal and *processual* through which we, as ethnographers, were able to encounter our humanity—thrownness, in this context, is affect itself. Phenomenologically, *thrownness* is the process through which humans encounter and are affected by the world: its joy, suffering, things, equipment, feelings, (mis)understanding, and techne. It is the process through which we figure things out for ourselves. But it is always in our encountering of the other, the other's face, the other's culture, that *thrownness* comes to the fore as an existential condition. In reflecting on our encounters with children and their parents from the three sites, London, Casablanca, and Beirut, we resisted the rigid institutionalised meaning-making structures that privilege 'objective' truth and 'empiricism' over process. The irony is that the two are inseparable. In fact, the *double-thrownness* we were at pains to explain was, for us, a source of critical reflection without which we may not have been able to modify our method. We championed *thrownness* as a process and let its affective structure guide both our ethnographic journey and our scientific pursuit. Our thrownness as ethnographers was traversal and processual. We have experienced its different facets in the field in an ontological way. But what unravelled for us was that this kind of encountering (being thrown and the messiness it produces) was what eventually gave birth to our critical and affective method. In this sense, and as we have already observed, ethnographic thrownness has a dual composition: it is at once an ontological condition and a thinking/figuring out process. While *being-thrown-in-the-world-ethnographically* is temporally finite, the figuring-things-out *process* it prompts is traversal. It really has no end point. Thrownness we need to add cannot be separated from the ethical events, produced by a collision between the objective world and affective regimes. Our thrownness was made the more difficult because of our implicatedness, first as Arab researchers who have both fled the Arab region for a more dignified and intellectually fulfilled existence and second as witnesses to a futural existence of an Arab generation, then children between the ages of 7 and 12, who are active and resourceful, but who also, to quote David Buckingham in our context, 'act under conditions that are not of their own choosing' (Buckingham 2008: 232).

Based on what we observed, witnessed and experienced in the three sites of the fieldwork, the future for a whole Arab generation does not breed optimism. Resourcefulness and the mnemonic imagination aside, the objective world of this whole Arab generation is fraught with conflict, war, sectarianism, dictatorship, cultural salafism, racism, and a public educational system that is intent on suffocating and stifling free and critical thinking, creativity, and individuality. It is this glimpse into the future that made our affective experiences in the field the more distressing.

The ethnographic method in the three cities allowed us to venture into the manifolds of children's worlds as much as they and their parents allowed us to. It gave us a close insight into the children's everydayness, their worldliness (in which media played an important part), and their narratives of selfhood. We designed the viewing holiday diaries to capture not only media uses but also the ways in which children's everyday lives were structured. We designed diary entries that taught us about the children's friendships, their emotions (how they felt on certain days and why), their houses, parents, religion, and socio-cultural habitus. The diaries had turned the intangible mediated familiar of children's everyday into a documented 'unfamiliar', allowing us and them to dialogically explore more folds to their worlds that we could not have otherwise captured. The diary entries did not only function as ethnographic prompts but were also in themselves the mediatic tools or equipment through which the children performed their worldliness and their being-in-the-world for us. In the case of London, children used the diaries to delineate a complex and mnemonic language, navigating between their Britishness/Londonness and their Arab heritage. The children mnemonically performed their identities in front of us (ethnographers of Arab origins) and in the presence of their parents through what we thought was a complex negotiation between Londonness, heritage and media as equipment. The parents were, as most first generations usually are, nostalgic about the past and their countries of origin and live therefore in a more linear cultural temporality. The children, however, were more at home with their Britishness, Londonness, and British media content. While their cultural temporal situatedness was by no means linear, they had a strong sense of a temporality that lied in the present cultural tense. Many have memorised whole lyrics from British *Grime* songs and talked with excitement about characters from British children's programming. While Arab TV channels were often on as we did the family observations, for many of the children of Arab origins living in the UK, these channels are tolerated as a constituent within the mnemonic, agential process of which they are in charge and as part of a cultural temporality that lives in the past at the levels of language and content. If anything, this reinforces the media phenomenology thesis—that media's care-structures are—in the first instance—inherent to their ability to mimic everyday structures. It is, as we learn from media phenomenology, through the media that our world and our everydayness are re-temporalised for us (Scannell 2014). In this sense, media uses of British-Arab children in the diaspora are more in tune culturally and temporally with the host country than they are with their parents' country of origin. So, while the children navigate mnemonically between different cultural temporalities (their parents' and theirs), the temporal distinction between these two identitarian repertoires is rather clear cut. While British cultural time, ceaselessly and intentionally reaffirmed through everyday mediatic structures, is situated in the present cultural tense, media content from the parents' countries of origin is out of sync with the children's everyday lives (at the level of language, popular culture, and structure of feeling) and cannot therefore form a coherent temporality for the children. *Incoherence* has to be read carefully in this context. We are not arguing that British children of Arab origin have no interest in their parents' cultural repertoire. Far from it, this repertoire is key to their worldliness and their identity formations. The point we are making, however, is that there is clear-cut distinction to be made at the temporal level. For the children, the British and Arab cultural repertoires reside in distinct and separate cultural temporalities. It is through the mnemonic process that they are brought together—a process over which the children have a lot of control.

Each fieldwork site threw different challenges at us. In Beirut, and especially in the case of the refugee family with whom we worked, the context of war was prevalent. Our positionality as researchers became entangled with ethical issues we had not anticipated. The family, literally all its members, confided in us. They trusted us enough to tell us their story of exile, marginalisation, and suffering. We had to do away with our pre-planned schema (the institutional demands of the academy) and listen most of the time. We had learnt very quickly that the children's media uses could not be understood outside the contexts of the Syrian war, Hezbollah's involvement, and the structural violence in the neighbourhood in which the children lived. That was their everyday. So, our role was blurred. In this context, we were ethnographers, social workers and activists all at the same time and this threw different methodological problems at us.

In our workshops in London, especially those we conducted in religious institutions such as mosques, Muslim community leaders as well as parents treated us at the beginning, and rightly so, with conspicuous mistrust. Why was it, they must have thought, that anyone would be interested in talking to Arab children in a cultural centre within a mosque about their media uses in a time when dozens of youngsters had pledged their allegiance to ISIS? The difficulty we encountered in accessing communities (the Moroccan and Lebanese and whose languages and cultural subtleties were familiar to us: both ethnographers having been born and bred in Lebanon and Morocco respectively) speaks volumes about the level of mistrust that exists between Muslim communities and the institution in the UK, be it media or the University. And why would the parents agree to give us access in a period of social British history that is fraught with islamophobia and fears of radicalisation? Once we had access, we had to think very carefully about how to engage the children in questions of identity, othering, gender, cultural time, and religiosity. A key workshop exercise we used across the three cities involved asking the children to design a one-week schedule for a new satellite channel aimed at Arab Children in the Arab world and in the diaspora. Initially, we used this exercise to assess levels of creativity, gender roles, othering, etc. This we found out quite a lot about, but we did not anticipate the strong links that existed between educational systems, conceptualisations of publicness and performing in such a workshop exercise. The children in the London workshops (who mostly went to state schools with the exception of one family that opted for home schooling) were the most organised, creative, and worked efficiently as groups out of all the children from the other sites. Children in the other two sites, Morocco and Lebanon, struggled with this exercise at the levels of both creativity and organisation. The schedules presented by Arab children in London showed a rich variety of programming, a lot of which we think was inspired (a) by an educational system where pupils are encouraged to work in groups and negotiate different roles and (b) a public service ethos that combined entertainment programming with current affairs such as news and documentary. Children in Morocco and in Lebanon were by contrast disorganised and unable to work efficiently within groups. Their schedules were merely copied from existing programmes. Even the children from middle-class households in these two sites who went to predominantly private schools lacked creativity and organisation in this exercise. What we inferred from this experiment is that the educational system in these two countries (Morocco and Lebanon), and we think it is safe to generalise and add the rest of the Arab world, is not conducive to encouraging individuality, negotiation, and creativity, nor is it conducive to, we need to add, critical thinking.

Un-concealing Children's *worldliness* be they in the UK, Morocco, or in Lebanon, required a comprehensive method that combined phenomenology's ruthless focus on visible phenomena with a type of questioning that can only come to the fore when visible phenomena are studied in wider structural contexts. To this end, this book thinks through, with and against media phenomenology. Our opting for a phenomenological method, unhinged by teleology or any discourse of becoming has, by default let us into, a methodological position, where invisible phenomena could simply not be ignored. Children's media uses in the Arab world today cannot be examined solely through a fundamentalist phenomenological approach. A critical phenomenology that is ready to engage with both visible and invisible phenomena is extremely crucial to producing a more contextualised and grounded knowledge on children and the media. While we agree that children's *worldliness* is a product of 'availableness', performativity, and affect, we also acknowledge that underlying this *worldliness* are invisible historical conditions that too need un-concealing. Arab children's *worldliness* is deeply implicated in savage, unorganised, neo-liberal structures that are continuously and indifferently privatising different facets of everyday life. These hidden phenomena, we argue, matter a lot to the current and future generations of Arabs and to delineating a critical approach for studying children and the media in the Arab world. Our non-media-centric approach to doing media studies has confirmed and reasserted for us a wisdom, arrived at by many before us, often neglected by media-centric approaches: context, context, context! To think against rather than with Heidegger this time, it is both visibility and hiddenness that characterise our world. Thinking with, through, and against phenomenology's default position for thinking about worldly phenomena has made it possible for us, methodologically, to first think outside sociology's hermeneutics in order for us to then reconnect with it, and here we mean its hermeneutics of suspicion.

Still at the level of method, our approach to the study of the everyday (children's everyday environment) was after a lot of grappling guided by a double-take: for us, the study of the everyday offered an opportunity to learn how children organised their routines, how their lives were implicated in everyday things, and how they performed being in the world as an everyday occurrence. We were interested in their daily uses of the media, how often they played out with friends, etc. However, as the research unfolded, we became aware of the different contexts in which discourses such as 'desnyfication', sectarianism, and cultural salafism had become entangled with children's everyday structures. Ideology is most dangerous and potent when it acquires ordinariness and becomes part of everyday cultural practices. In the case of Beirut, children's everyday lives, their media uses included, were deeply entrenched in discourses of sectarianism. In Morocco where Sectarianism is non-existent, some children between 7 and 12 have openly denounced Shiism, Christianity, and Judaism as a deviation from the true faith and did not hesitate to speak of these faiths negatively. In the case of Morocco, a country renowned for its moderate and tolerant Islam, it is clear from our conversations with children from the working classes, especially, that cultural Salafist ideology is gaining ground there. Our double-take in engaging with the everyday combined the culturalist approach with ideology critique. We are especially inspired by Raymond Williams who took the everyday and lived experience as the ground for a conscious and reflective analysis of culture. But we have also taken our cue from Stuart Hall's two paradigms approach to doing cultural studies (1980). Thus, our attempt to also grapple with the wider and underlying everyday structures that remain dangerously hidden: cultural salafism and neo-liberal forces being two key examples. Reducing configurations of everyday life to media is also problematic, as it limits it to the realm of the institutional. Everyday life, as we have deduced from this research, is a far more complex and varied phenomenon.

## ON THE QUESTION OF ARABNESS

The ethnographic evidence points to a clear disjunction between 'Arabness' as a discursive, pan-Arabist narrative and 'Arabness' as a structure of feeling about the world. In the case of Morocco, we learnt how the majority of the children identified more with Moroccanness and Islam than they did with being Arab, that is, even if half of the population is of an Arab origin. Arabness for the children of Casablanca was closely associated with language, or how Arabic is spoken. Arabness for the children denoted countries of the Gulf, Egypt, and countries of the Levant. The children understood that Arabic was the language of the Koran, and that by default God spoke the same language, making it a sacred, and transcendental language. This sacredness, however, did not translate at the level of belonging or at the level of structures of feeling. The language of the Koran is just that—sacred, Semitic, and transcendental—it has no relation to their everyday, spoken Moroccan-Arabic. From a mediatic perspective, Arabness can be translated at the level of regionalisation, and the political economy of the Arab media. For a long time, when Egypt led the Arab region between the 1950 and 1980s at the level of cultural production (especially cinema and later television), Arabness as discourse became strongly associated with Egyptianness. This role was claimed from Qatar through its satellite channel Aljazeera whose role transcended the remit of Arabic news production to an intentional and discursive attempt at reviving the pan-Arab identitarian project, this time with an Islamist flavour. It is no wonder Aljazeera put a huge effort to tap into Arab children audiences, a project which failed because of reasons we do not have the luxury of space to engage with in this concluding chapter. At the linguistic level, Aljazeera were committed through their news broadcasts (with news readers from different regions of the Arab world) to standardise Arabic (Al-Jazeera Arabic) as a common frame and language. While Al-Jazeera helped children from Morocco to sympathise with the children in Gaza and the occupied territories, Al-Jazeera, as a Pan-Arab project, never cohered with the children's structures of feelings at the identitarian level because it failed to speak the language of *shaa'b* (people), the language of popular culture, and let us be precise: the language of the present cultural tense. The pan-Arabist project and what was left of it was then totally obliterated by Saudi Arabia through its MBC empire and its ruthless complicity with the US's cultural imperialism project. The new pan-Arabism, led by Saudi Arabia's MBC, is a mere vehicle for American soft power and for the ruling elite in Saudi Arabia. The new Pan-Arabism, or shall we say 'Pan-Arab-Disneyism', is a business and has to be understood from a political economy perspective as such. It is devoid of any ethics or vision. It is a bourgeois, neo-liberal fraud.

Lebanon is known for its pluralist political and permissive social climate, turning into the battle scene of conflicting national, regional, and international powers, as well as the playground for tourism and entertainment. Its proximity and history of close involvement in the Palestinian cause led to one of the earliest and bloodiest civil wars in the regions. At the time of the fieldwork, it was also suffocating under an unprecedented environmental crisis due to the corruption of national waste management bodies. Most importantly, it was bearing the humanitarian heaviest burden of the Syrian conflict among other Arab countries, receiving the highest number of Syrian refugees in the region. Lebanon, historically known for its high educational and diasporic capital, is also the earliest Arab countries to adapt neo-liberal policies in the aftermath of the civil war (1975–1990), which have depleted local markets and widened the skills capital between rich and poor, and the metropolis of Beirut and the peripheries. It is no surprise that the majority of the population relies on remittances from relatives living abroad. These layers of complexities bring a fractured historical, political, and social climate where at once anything goes and nothing is resolved. Pan-Arabism in Lebanon has been controversial, with its national policies characterised as turning one eye to the Palestinian cause, and the other eye on a desirable affinity with Western cultural production. Beyond the divisions of different political and military factions over the Palestinian and Syrian conflicts, national policies in Lebanon are of cultural enmeshment, characterised with a bi-lingual (and sometimes trilingual) educational system, a privatised health system, a Swiss-style banking haven for regional capital, and open markets. It was also one of the first countries to open up to globalised satellite media production and consumption. It is within this context that children in Lebanon are growing up, engaging with a toxic mix of sectarianism, corruption, environmental suffocation, racism, and deprivation. At the everyday level, these issues are sensed but not uttered. They form a backdrop of unease and volatility that is detected through a childhood malaise of identity formation. Arabness in Lebanon was absent from both the discourses and enactment of children and their families. At the level of language, middle-class

Lebanese children—including those residing in Lebanon and those in the diasporic Gulf region—did not speak in Arabic, instead making a point to switch the language of conversation into American English. It was a sign that the country has moved away from its francophone history and has embraced Americanism as the desirable mode of a 'modern' cultural existence. Their fascination with American English was directly connected not only to the American satellite channels such as the Disney Channel, Nickolodeon, and MBC, but also to the intertextuality between these shows and a social desirability to be 'Western' (read modern) in opposition to 'parochial' defined in the use of Arabic language and Arabic-speaking media. Middle-class children's worldliness was synonymous to 'Westernness', manifested in their fondness of international cuisine and Western celebrity pop culture. Unlike children in the other fieldwork sites, their time schedule was tightly controlled by their parents, who encouraged them to watch 'good content' like DVDs of Disney classics and new hits, in addition to visiting Western-style themed parks, such as KidzMondo, a neo-liberal entertainment venture replicating a functioning city, where children take on different labour roles ranging from working at a gas station, as a hotel cleaner, a baker, or a banker. These activities coincided with children's fondness for video games such as SimCity, that is devised for children to build an entire city from scratch and populate it with inhabitants, or which one respondent explained as 'it's like being God'. These experiences sat side by side with uncomfortable truths about the acute deprivation of Syrian and Palestinian refugee children, who faced everyday racism and ostracisation from the overstretched and inadequate humanitarian provision, leaving them hanging in the dissonance of the rhetoric of 'Arab solidarity' that is touted by various conflicting political parties.

## On Media as *Equipment*

Our ethnographic research uncovered varied and complex media uses by the children in the three sites. We borrowed Heidegger's concept 'equipment' to unpack children's media uses because, as a concept, it captured the functional ways in which the children used the media. Functional uses of the media by the children enabled them to extend beyond the confines of their material realities. Media, as we learned from ethnography, were *the equipment* through which topographies of being and the imagination were extended. Media made it possible, especially for children from poorer working-class backgrounds, to be part of a more expansive worldliness. Equipment, as we explained, is equated with 'serviceability, conduciveness, usability and manipulability' (Heidegger 1962: 970). We showed how in the cases of Casablanca, children from very poor families carved out (*disclosing* and *discovering*) new spatio-temporal geographies of being and encountering that transcended the alienating confinements of their everyday material lives. Media as equipment unveiled different types of functionality at the level of uses. Across the three sites, the children used the media as equipment to construct narratives of self; they did this performatively through ontologising media and its varied texts in ways that turned them into bodily objects. Children did not just speak about the media, they spoke through the media. Media were also part of an imaginative, mnemonic process, and were functionally used by the children to navigate between the cultural repertoires of different generations. It was these ethnographic findings surrounding the functionality of the media as equipment which pushed us to rethink the whatness of media beyond its conventional definition of broadcasting/digitality/screen/computer that separates the media text and its audience into distinct entities. Instead, we were invited to accommodate a more anthropo-centric vision of media uses that considers forms of media as an extended anthropo-centric bodily structure where bodily organs become extended forms of technicity and where, as we learn from Andre Leroi-Gourhan (1964) and Gilbert Simondon (2018), media and technology become extensions of our humanity.

As we went along with the fieldwork, it became apparent that the anthropo-centric nature of technicity was speaking to a new technological era fusing human bodies and media objects into a hybrid mediated existence where technology is not only part of children's lives, but are constituent of their experiences of their world, both physically and phantasmagorically. While established works remained focused on the broadcasting model which assumes a separation between the sender of the message and the recipient audiences, children came across as 'equipped' users who used media objects as an extension of their daily practices. Far from being passive recipients of entertainment or even 'edutainment', children did not care much for the institutional sources producing content. Instead, they approached various media as a source of knowledge about the world, getting in direct connection with popularised knowledge on platforms such as Facebook and YouTube. It is sobering to acknowledge that children in the Arab region will be relying less and less on institutionalised knowledge production through schooling or broadcast media, and more on their own fractal assemblages of meaning-making that they derive through their deep un-institutional connections with the bottomless and limitless realm of the digital world.

It is within the intersections of un-institutional realms of digitality, multiple social spaces, temporalities, and socialities that children formed their worlds. They weaved a multidimensional web-like network of connections that they moved across. In each context, these intersections shaped intricate identities that they negotiated in the school (London), the *Derb* or neighbourhood (Casablanca), and the extended family (Beirut).

The Home emerged as a spatial-temporal hub hosting these intersections. It was modelled by various forces beyond the socio-economic situation of the household. The spatial organisation of the household and living arrangements affected children's media use across classes and contexts. Significantly, the informal negotiation of hierarchies within the family, along with the parents' pedagogic, cultural, and political ideals, regulated children's access to and control over their media use. However, children rose as astute negotiators of media use, benefiting from a technological advantage over their elder generations who are still hung on the TV as primary communal device of media uses and which is still dominant in epistemologies on Arabic-speaking children today.

The centrality of the TV as the omnipresent medium was destabilised. Children moved between devices and platforms in complex assemblages of communicability that included watching programmes, playing games, and socialising through social media. Children did not follow the model of conversion. Their engagement was deeply affective, reflecting elaborate processes of bricolage of content and meaning through different media and devices.

The phone came out as a coveted object of affection that transcended availability to presence. Regardless of its availability, it appealed to children and occupied their imaginaries. The phone was in full presence across the most affluent and poorest households alike. Across the three sites, the phone was a rite of passage, a marker of 'growing up'. It symbolised an individual independent state of being-in-the-world transporting them to an aspired pre-adulthood. The phone was a portal to an affective-epistemological being-doing connecting children to the many associative connections they made with their physical and social environment.

## BIBLIOGRAPHY

Buckingham, D. (2008). Children and Media: A Cultural Studies Approach. In S. Livingstone & K. Drotner (Eds.), *The International Handbook of Children, Media and Culture*. London: Sage.

Heidegger, M. (1962). *Being and Time*. London: Blackwell.

Leroi-Gourhan, A. (1964). *Le geste et la parole*. Paris: éditions albin michel.

Scannell, P. (2014). *Television and the Meaning of the Live: An Enquiry into the Human Situation*. Cambridge: Polity.

Simondon, G. (2018). *On the Mode of Existence of Technical Objects* (C. Malsapina & J. Rogove, Trans.). London: Univocal.

# BIBLIOGRAPHY

Adorno, T., & Horkheimer, M. (1944). The Culture Industry: Enlightenment as Mass Deception. In T. Adorno & M. Horkheimer (Eds.), *Dialectics of Enlightenment* (J. Cumming, Trans.). New York: Herder and Herder, 1972.

Alasuutari, P. (1999). Introduction: Three Phases of Reception Studies. In P. Alasuutari (Ed.), *Rethinking the Media Audience*. London: Sage.

al-Mesfer, M. (n.d.). Tahlil al-risala al-iʿlamiya: Taʾthir al-fadaʾiyat al-ʿarabiyya ʿala alshabab al-ʿarabi ['Analysis of the Media Message: The effect of Arab Satellite Channels on Arab Youth']. *al-Mufakkir Journal, 3*, 31–61.

al-Salmi, L., & Smith, P. H. (2015). The Digital Biliteracies of Arab Immigrant Mothers. *Literacy Research: Theory, Method, and Practice, 64*, 193–209.

Amezaga Albizu, J. (2007). Geolinguistic Regions and Diasporas in the Age of Satellite Television. *International Communication Gazette, 69*(3), 239–261.

Ang, I. (1985). *Watching Dallas: Soap Opera and the Melodramatic Imagination*. London: Methuen.

Awan, F. (2016). *Occupied Childhoods: Discourses and Politics of Childhood and Their Place in Palestinian and Pan-Arab Screen Content for Children* (Ph.D. thesis). University of Westminster.

Banaji, S. (2017). *Children and Media in India: Narratives of Class, Agency, and Social Change*. New York: Routledge.

Barad, K. (2007). *Meeting the Universe Halfway: Quantum Physics and the Entanglement of Matter and Meaning*. London: Duke University Press.

Barker, J. (2009). Introduction: Ethnographic Approaches to the Study of Fear. *Anthropologica, 51*(2), 237–267.

Benbassa, E. (2010). *Suffering as Identity: The Jewish Paradigm*. London: Verso.

Bhabha, H. (1994). *The Location of Culture*. London: Routledge.

Bird, S. E. (2003). *The Audience in Everyday Life*. London: Routledge.

© The Editor(s) (if applicable) and The Author(s) 2019
T. Sabry and N. Mansour, *Children and Screen Media in Changing Arab Contexts*, https://doi.org/10.1007/978-3-030-04321-6

Bird Rose, D. (1996). *Nourishing Terrains: Australian Aboriginal Views of Landscape and Wilderness*. Canberra: Australian Heritage Commission.

Bolognani, M. (2007). Islam, Ethnography and Politics: Methodological Issues in Researching amongst West Yorkshire Pakistanis in 2005. *International Journal of Social Research Methodology*, 10(4), 279–293.

Boltanski, L. (1999). *Distant Suffering: Morality Media and Politics*. Cambridge: Cambridge University Press.

Bourdieu, P. (1984). *Distinction: A Social Critique of the Judgment of Taste*. London: Routledge.

Buckingham, D. (Ed.). (2002). *Small Screens: television for Children* (pp. 38–60). Leicester: Leicester University Press.

Buckingham, D. (2007). Selling Childhood: Children and Consumer Culture. *Journal of Children and Media, 1*(1), 15–24. https://doi.org/10.1080/17482790601005017.

Buckingham, D. (2008). Children and Media: A Cultural Studies Approach. In S. Livingstone & K. Drotner (Eds.), *The International Handbook of Children, Media and Culture*. London: Sage.

Buckingham, D., & Bragg, S. (2004). *Young People, Sex and the Media: The Facts of Life*. London: Palgrave Macmillan.

Buckingham, D., & Sefton-green, J. (1994). *Cultural Studies Goes to School: Reading and Teaching Popular Culture*. London: Taylor and Francis.

Buckingham, D., et al. (1999). *Children's Television Britain: History, Discourse and Policy*. London: British Film institute.

Buijzen, M., van der Molen, J. W., & Sondij, P. (2007). Parental Mediation of Children's Emotional Responses to a Violent News Event. *Communication Research, 34*(2), 212–230.

Butler, J. (1990). *Gender Trouble: Feminism and the Subversion of Identity*. New York: Routledge.

Chatterjee, P. (1993). *The Nation and Its Fragments: Colonial and Postcolonial Histories*. Princeton: Princeton University Press.

Chatty, D., et al. (2014). *Ensuring Quality Education for Young Refugees from Syria (12–25 Years): A Mapping Exercise* (RSC Research Report, 2014). http://www.rsc.ox.ac.uk/files/publications/other/rr-syria-youth-education-2014.pdf.

Christensen, P., & James, A. (Eds.). (2000). *Conducting Research with Children*. London: Falmer Press.

Critcher, C. (2008). Making Waves: Historical Aspects of Public Debates About Children and Mass Media. In S. Livingstone & K. Drtoner (Eds.), *International Handbook of Children, Media and Culture* (pp. 91–104). London: Sage.

Cunningham, H. (1995). *Children and Childhood in Western Society Since 1500*. London: Longman.

Das, V. (1985). Anthropological Knowledge and Collective Violence: The Riots in Delhi, November 1984. *Anthropology Today, 1*(3), 4–6.

Das, V. (1990). Our Work to Cry: Your Work to Listen. In V. Das (Ed.), *Mirrors of Violence* (pp. 345–399). Oxford: Oxford University Press.

Das, V. (Ed.). (1990). *Mirrors of Violence*. Oxford: Oxford University Press.

Das, V., Kleinman, A., Ramphele, M., & Reynolds, P. (2002). *Violence and Subjectivity*. Berkeley and Los Angeles: University of California Press.

Dashty. (2010). Athar Mushahadat Al Baramij Al Fada'iya `ala Al Al Maharat Al Ijtima`iya lil Tofl Al Arabi [The Effects of Watching Satellite Channels on the Social Skills of the Arab Child].

Deacon, R., & Parker, B. (1995). Education as Subjection and Refusal: An Elaboration on Foucault. *Curriculum Studies, 3*(2), 109–122.

Dorsky, S., & Stevenson, B. T. (1995). Childhood and Education in Highland North Yemen. In E. Fenea (Ed.), *Children in the Muslim Middle East* (pp. 309–324). Austin: University of Text Press.

Dover, C. (2007). Everyday Talk: Investigating Media Uses and Identity Amongst School Children. *Particip@tions, 4*(1).

Dreyfus, L. H. (1991). *Being-in-the World: A Commentary on Heidegger's Being and Time Division 1*. London: MIT Press.

Drotner, K. (1999). Dangerous Media? Panic Discourses. *Paedogogica Historica, 35*(3), 593–619.

Fabian, J. (1983). *Time and The Other*. New York: Columbia University Press.

Foucault, M. (1978). Governmentality. In G. Burchell, C. Gordon, & P. Miller (Eds.), *The Foucault Effect: Studies in Governmentality* (pp. 87–104). London: Harvester Wheatsheaf.

Fuchs, C. (2016). *Critical Theory of Communication*. London: University of Westminster Press.

Fuchs, C. (2017). *Social Media: A Critical Introduction* (2nd ed.). London: Sage.

Garnham, N., & Williams, R. (1980). Pierre Bourdieu and the Sociology of Culture: An Introduction. *Media, Culture and Society, 2*(3), 209–223.

Gittins, D. (2009). The Historical Construction of Childhood. In M. J. Kehily (Ed.), *An Introduction to Childhood Studies* (2nd ed., pp. 35–49). Maidenhead, UK and New York: Open University Press.

Haboush, K. (2007). Working with Arab American Families: Culturally Competent Practice for School Psychologists. *Psychology in the Schools, 44*(2), 183–198.

Hall, S. (1980). Cultural Studies: Two Paradigms. *Media, Culture and Society, 2*, 57–72.

Hannerz, U. (1992). *Cultural Complexity: Studies in the Social Organization of Meaning*. New York: Columbia University Press.

Harb, Z., & Bessaiso, E. (2006). British Arab Muslim Audiences and Television After September 11. *Journal of Ethnic and Migration Studies, 32*(6), 1063–1076.

Heidegger, M. (1962). *Being and Time.* London: Blackwell.

Heidegger, M. (1992). *The Concept of Time: The First Draft of Being and Time.* London: Continuum.

Hendrick, H. (1997). Constructions and Reconstructions of British Childhood: An Interpretive Survey, 1800 to the Present. In A. James & A. Prout (Eds.), *Constructing and Reconstructing Childhood: Contemporary Issues in the Sociological Study of Childhood* (pp. 34–62). London: Falmer Press.

Hobsbawm, E. (1991). Exile. *Social Research, 58*(1), 67–68.

Hyers, L., Swim, J., & Mallet, R. (2006). The Personal Is Political: Using Daily Diaries to Examine Everyday Prejudice-Related Experiences. In S. Hesse-Biber & P. Leavy (Eds.), *Emergent Methods in Social Research.* London: Sage.

James, A. (1993). *Childhood Identities. Self and Social Relationships in the Experience of the Child.* Edinburgh: Edinburgh University Press.

James, A. (2001). Ethnography in the Study of Children and Childhood. In P. Atkinson, A. Coffey, S. Delamont, J. Lofland, & I. Lofland (Eds.), *Handbook of Ethnography* (pp. 246–257). London: Sage.

Jamieson, L., Simpson, R., & Lewis, R. (2012). *Researching Families and Relationships: Reflections on Process.* London: Palgrave.

Jenks, C. (2009). Constructing Childhood Sociologically. In M. J. Kehily (Ed.), *An Introduction to Childhood Studies* (2nd ed., pp. 93–111). Maidenhead, UK and New York: Open University Press.

Keightley, E., & Pickering, M. (2012). *The Mnemonic Imagination: Remembering as Creative Practice.* London: Palgrave.

King, A. (2000). Thinking with Bourdieu Against Bourdieu: A Practical Critique of the Habitus. *Sociological Theory, 18*(3), 417–433.

Kleinman, A. (2002). The Violences of Everyday Life: The Multiple forms and Dynamics of social Violence. In V. Das, A. Kleinman, M. Ramphele, & P. Reynolds (Eds.), *Violence and Subjectivity.* Berkeley and Los Angeles: University of California Press.

Kovacic, Z., & Karamat, P. (2005). An Alternative Measure of the Digital Divide between Arab Countries. In *Proceedings of the Second International Conference on Innovations in Information Technology.* Dubai: United Arab Emirates University College of Information Technology.

Latour, B. (2005). *Reassembling the Social: An Introduction to Actor-Network-Theory.* Oxford: Oxford University Press.

Lazovsky, R. (2007). Educating Jewish and Arab Children for Tolerance and Coexistence in a Situation of Ongoing Conflict: An Encounter Program. *Cambridge Journal of Education, 37*(3), 391–408.

Lemish, D., & Götz, M. (Eds.). (2007). *Children and Media in Times of Conflict and War*. NJ: Hampton press.

Lemish, D., & Pick-Alony, R. (2014). Inhabiting Two Worlds: The Role of News in the Lives of Jewish and Arab Children and Youth in Israel. *International Communication Gazette, 76*(2), 128–151.

Leroi-Gourhan, A. (1964). *Le geste et la parole*. Paris: éditions albin michel.

Leurs, K. (2015). *Digital Passages: Migrant Youth 2.0: Diaspora, Gender and Youth Cultural Intersections*. Amsterdam: Amsterdam University Press.

Levinas, E. (1998). *Entre Nous, Thinking of-the-Other*. New York: Columbia University Press.

Lippitt, J. (2003). *Kierkegaard and Fear and Trembling*. New York: Routledge.

Livingstone, S. (2002). *Young People and New Media*. London: Sage.

Livingstone, S. (2007). From Family Television To Bedroom Culture: Young People's Media At Home. In E. Devereux (Ed.), *Media Studies: Key Issues and Debates* (pp. 302–321). London, UK: Sage.

Livingstone, S., Haddon, L., & Gorzig, A. (Eds.). (2012). *Children, Risk and Safety on the Internet*. London: Polity Press.

Livingstone, S., Haddon, L., Vincent, J., Mascheroni, G., & Ólafsson, K. (2014). *Net Children Go Mobile: The UK Report*. Milan, Italy.

Mansour, N. (2018). Unmaking the Arab/Muslim Child: Lived Experiences of Media Use in Two Migratory Settings. *Middle East Journal of Culture and Communication, 11*(1), 91–110.

Mansour, N., & Sabry, T. (2017). (Mis)trust, Access and the Poetics of Self-Reflexivity: Arab Diasporic Children in London and Media Consumption. In N. Sakr & J. Steemers (Eds.), *Children's Tv and Digital Media in the Arab World: Childhood, Screen Culture and Education* (pp. 207–226). London: I.B. Tauris.

Marcus, G. E. (1995). Ethnography in/of the World System: The Emergence of Multi-Sited Ethnography. *Annual Review of Anthropology, 24*, 95–117.

Marshall, J. D. (1989). Foucault and Education. *Australian Journal of Education, 33*(2), 99–113.

Matar, D. (2006). Diverse Diasporas, One Meta-Narrative: Palestinians in the UK Talking About 11 September 2001. *Journal of Ethnic and Migration Studies, 32*(6), 1027–1040.

Mcluhan, M. ([1994] 1964). *Understanding Media: The Extensions of Man*. Cambridge: MIT Press.

Medin, D. L. (1994). *Psychology of Learning and Motivation: Advances in Research and Theory* (p. 227). San Diego, CA: Academic Press.

Meer, N. (2007). Muslim Schools in Britain: Challenging Mobilisations or Logical Developments? *Asia Pacific Journal of Education, 27*(1), 55–71.

Messenger Davies, M. (2008). Studying Children's Television (Goodnight Mr. Tom). In G. Creeber (Ed.), *The Television Genre Book* (pp. 92–97). London: Palgrave Macmillan.

Michaels, E. (1986). *The Aboriginal Invention of Television in Central Australia 1982–1986.* Canberra: Australian Institute of Aboriginal Studies.

Miladi, N. (2006). Satellite Television News and the Arab Diaspora in Britain: Comparing al-Jazeera, the BBC and CNN. *Journal of Ethnic and Migration Studies, 32*(6), 947–960.

Moores, S. (1993). *Interpreting Audiences: The Ethnography of Media Consumption.* London: Sage.

Morley, D. (1980). *The Nationwide Audience.* London: British Film Institute.

Morley, D. (1986). *Family Television: Cultural Power and Domestic Leisure.* London: Comedia.

Morley, D. (1992). *Television Audiences and Cultural Studies.* London: Routledge.

Morley, D. (2000). *Home Territories Media, Mobility and Identity.* London: Comedia.

Nuttall, Sarah. (2009). *Entanglement, Literary and Cultural Reflections on Post-Apartheid.* Johannesburg: Wits University Press.

Ofcom. (2017). *Children and Parents: Media Use and Attitudes Report.* www.ofcom.org.uk/__data/assets/pdf_file/0020/108182/children-parents-media-use-attitudes-2017.pdf.

Olwig, K. F., & Gulløv, E. (2003). Towards an Anthropology of Children and Place. In K. F. Olwig & E. Gulløv (Eds.), *Children's Places, Cross-Cultural Perspectives* (pp. 1–22). London: Routledge.

Peters, D. J. (2015). *The Marvellous Clouds: Toward a Philosophy of Elemental Media.* London: University of Chicago Press.

Pike, K. (2018). Disney in Doha Arab Girls Negotiate Global and Local Versions of Disney Media. *The Middle East Journal of Culture and Communication, 11*(1), 72–90.

Pink, S. (2013). *Doing Visual Ethnography* (2nd ed.). London: Sage.

Pink, S. (2015). *Doing Sensory Ethnography* (2nd ed.). London: Sage.

Projansky, S. (2014). *Spectacular Girls: Media Fascination and Celebrity Culture.* New York: New York University Press.

Punch, S. (2002). Research with Children: The Same or Different from Research with Adults? *Childhood, 9*(3), 321–341.

Radway, J. (1984). *Reading the Romance: Women, Patriarchy, and Popular Literature.* Philadelphia: University of Pennsylvania Press.

Rinnawi, K. (2012). 'Instant Nationalism' and the 'Cyber Mufti': The Arab Diaspora in Europe and the Transnational Media. *Journal of Ethnic and Migration Studies, 38*(9), 1451–1467. https://doi.org/10.1080/1369183X.2012.698215.

Rodman, G. (2004). *Media in a Changing World: History, Industry.* Controversy: McGraw-Hill.

Rogers, A., Casey, M., Ekert, J., & Holland, J. (2005). Interviewing Children Using an Interpretive Poetics. In S. Greene & D. Hogan (Eds.), *Researching Children's Experience: Approaches and Methods*. London: Sage.

Sabry, T. (2007). An interview with Paddy Scannell. *Westminster Papers in Communication and Culture, 4*(2), 3–23.

Sabry, T. (2010). *Cultural Encounters in the Arab World: On the Media, The Modern and the Everyday*. London: I.B. Tauris.

Sabry, T. (2019). Cultural Time and Everyday Life in the Middle Atlas Mountain Village of Ait Nuh. In T. Sabry & J. F. Khalil (Eds.), *Culture, Time and Publics in the Arab World*. London: I.B. Tauris.

Sakr, N. (2002). *Satellite Realms: Transnational Television, Globalisation and the Middle East*. London: I.B. Tauris.

Sakr, N. (2007). *Arab Television Today*. London: I.B. Tauris.

Saloom, R. (2005). I Know You Are, but What Am I? Arab-American Experiences Through the Critical Race Theory Lens. *Hamline Journal of Public Law & Policy, 27*(1), 55–76.

Scannell, P. (2014). *Television and the Meaning of the Live: An Enquiry into the Human Situation*. Cambridge: Polity.

Scourfield, J., Gilliat-Ray, S., Khan, A., & Otri, S. (2013). *Muslim Childhood: Religious Nurture in a European Context*. Oxford: Oxford University Press.

Simondon, G. (2018). *On the Mode of Existence of Technical Objects* (C. Malsapina & J. Rogove, Trans.). London: Univocal.

Slone, M., Shechner, T., & Khoury, O. F. (2011). Parenting Style as a Moderator of Effects of Political Violence: Cross-Cultural Comparison of Israeli Jewish and Arab Children. *International Journal of Behavioral Development, 36*(1), 62–70.

Sontag, S. (2003). *Regarding the Pain of Others*. New York: Picador.

Stolcke, V. (1995). Talking Culture: New Boundaries, New Rhetoric of Exclusion in Europe. *Current Anthropology, 36*(3), 1–13.

Sundas, A. (2008). *Second and Third Generation Muslims in Britain: A Socially Excluded Group?* Identities, Integration and Community Cohesion (Oxford). http://www.wjh.harvard.edu/~hos/papers/Sundas%20Ali.pdf.

Svendsen, L. (2008). *A Philosophy of Fear*. London: Reaktion Books.

Tayie, S. (2008). *Children and Mass Media in the Arab World: A Second Level Analysis UNESCO*. https://milunesco.unaoc.org/mil-articles/children-and-mass-media-in-the-arab-world-a-second-level-analysis-2/.

Watkins, K. (2013). *Education Without Borders: A Summary. A Report from Lebanon on Syria's Out of School Children*. Overseas Development Institute.

Weber, M. (2015). The Distribution of Power with the Gemeinschaft: Classes, *Stände*, Parties. In D. Waters & T. Waters (Eds. and Trans.) *Weber''s Rationalism and Modern Society: New Translations on Politics, Bureaucracy and Social Stratification*. New York: Palgrave Macmillan.

World Bank. (2017). *Staff Estimates Using the World Bank's Total Population and Age/Sex Distributions of the United Nations Population Division's World Population Prospects: 2017 Revision.* https://data.worldbank.org/indicator/SP.POP.0014.TO?locations=1A&year_high_desc=false.

Zeitlyn, B., & Mand, K. (2012). Researching Transnational Childhoods. *Journal of Ethnic and Migration Studies, 38*(6), 987–1006. https://doi.org/10.1080/1369183X.2012.677179.

## FIELD NOTES

Creative Workshop 1, London, October, 2013.
Creative Workshop 2, London, October, 2013.
Creative Workshop 4, Casablanca, July, 2014.
Creative Workshop 5, Casablanca, July, 2014.
Creative Workshop 6, Casablanca, August, 2014.
Creative workshop 8, Beirut, August, 2015.
Creative Workshop 9, Beirut, August, 2015.
Ethnography 1, London, July, 2013.
Ethnography 2, London, July, 2013.
Ethnography 3, London, July, 2013.
Ethnography 4, London, July, 2013.
Ethnography 5, Casablanca, July, 2014.
Ethnography 6, Casablanca, July, 2014.
Ethnography 7, Casablanca, July, 2014.
Ethnography 9, Lebanon, August, 2015.
Ethnography 10, Beirut, August, 2015.
Ethnography 11, Beirut, August, 2015.

# INDEX

© The Editor(s) (if applicable) and The Author(s) 2019
T. Sabry and N. Mansour, *Children and Screen Media in Changing Arab Contexts*, https://doi.org/10.1007/978-3-030-04321-6

143

GPSR Compliance
The European Union's (EU) General Product Safety Regulation (GPSR) is a set
of rules that requires consumer products to be safe and our obligations to
ensure this.

If you have any concerns about our products, you can contact us on

ProductSafety@springernature.com

In case Publisher is established outside the EU, the EU authorized
representative is:

Springer Nature Customer Service Center GmbH
Europaplatz 3
69115 Heidelberg, Germany